Your Brilliant
Un-Career

Women,
Entrepreneurship,
and Making the Leap

Cas McCullough

Published 2014 by Just One Thing Press
PO Box 7193
Mount Crosby Q 4306
Australia

E: cas@casmccullough.com
W: casmccullough.com and yourbrilliantuncareer.com

Illustrations: Caroline McCullough
Cover Design: Natalie Soupronovich, Caroline McCullough and Paul Gleave
Book Design: Paul Gleave

ISBN: 978-0-9872432-3-2

Subjects: Business and Economics

Edition One December 2014

Please note that while Internet links were tested at the time of publishing, they may change or disappear in the future. Please report any broken links to cas@casmccullough.com.

For Liam, Daniel and Adam

May you always believe you can reach for the stars!

Acknowledgements

This book would not have happened without the encouragement of my friend and business colleague Amanda Foy, who said, "You have so much knowledge stored in that brain of yours, you should write a book". And I'd like to thank my editor Alex Mitchell, who helped me bring this book to life and Paul Gleave for making the layout incredible!

I would also like to acknowledge my accountability buddy in 2012, Stacey Myers, and my 2012 life coach Kerri Baruch—you both impacted on this book more than you know. Thanks to the inspirational Mari Smith who first introduced me to the 'one to many' principal; May King Tsang for her constant praise and encouragement; Annemarie Cross for being an excellent mentor and for showing me how to harness my strengths to create my dream business; author Sally Thibault for not only reading an early draft of this book and providing incredible feedback within about 48 hours of me sending her the manuscript, but for re-reading a later draft, editing it and writing the Foreword... words just can't express how grateful I am. A massive thank you to the 22 amazing women who contributed their stories to this book: Krishna Everson, Dana D'Orsi, Nitty Brown, Natalie Souprounovich, Amanda Hoffmann, May King Tsang, Janine Evans, Agimary Joseph, Chris Wildeboer, Robin Hardy, Meredith Eisenberg, Debbie Hatswell, Mary Gardam, Celena Ross, Dhea Bartlett, Christine Smith, Susan Popovski, Linda Reed-Enever, Hazel Theocharous, Jane Del Rosso, Nicole Leedham and Jan Muir. Thanks also to Shar Moore, Bec Derrington, Alison Vidotto, Dan Norris, Matthew Dunstan, Annemarie Cross (again), Adam Franklin, Donna Hamer, Joshua Clifton, Phil McGregor and Sally Thibault (again) for contributing their expertise in the bonus interviews that go with this book.

Thank you to Kathi Cooper Laughman and Alison Dias Laverty for their feedback on the first completed draft, and Phil McGregor for helping me brainstorm collaboration ideas for chapter ten and for making me laugh a lot over the past few months. Thanks to Des Evans for allowing me to use his business as an example in the branding chapter. Thanks to Katrina Graham for helping me brainstorm ideas for the subtitle. A huge thank you to friends Melissa, Anthea, Marieke, Anna, Karsten, Aaron, Erica, and Ali for being there for me while I was writing, and helping me process some of the personal stuff that's in this book and much of the personal stuff that isn't. Thanks to my sister Becky for taking the time to read the manuscript and candidly share her viewpoint as a corporate executive. A massive thank you to my clients and my team! Without you I could not have stepped off the corporate ladder to do the fun and amazing work I do. Also, a huge thank you to Kati Krebs, my midwife friend who may just have saved my life by walking into the room when she did.

Thanks to my children Liam, Daniel and Adam. They've been incredibly patient with me throughout this process. Also, thanks to Wayne who has journeyed with me through much of this.

One last thank you. I thank God for giving me the gift of being able to put my thoughts into words, and for giving me such a rich and amazing life. I am incredibly blessed!

Preface

When I was seven months pregnant with my first child (who's now a teenager), I was working for a state government department in Australia as a contract communication executive. It was nothing riveting really. I wrote press releases about government-funded toilets and oversaw annual report publishing, stuff like that.

One day my boss was interviewing people to fill one of the roles in our department, and when one of the interviewees left, my boss turned around and said: "Well, she's qualified, but she's been a stay-at-home mum for seven years, and is just trying to get back into the workforce. I don't think she'll be suitable."

I made a mental note that day: 'women who take time out from work will be disadvantaged.' The woman was a former journalist, more than qualified to write press releases about toilet blocks, but because she had left her job to raise her family, she was considered 'not suitable'. That left me feeling a bit scared about my future. Would I too be discriminated against when I took time out to raise my family? I left that position to have my first baby, and rather than take the risk that I'd be seen as unqualified, I kept working, on and off, as a freelance consultant, a part-time research assistant at a university and eventually left these roles behind to set up my own enterprise.

Much has changed for women in the past few years. Back in the late 1990s I wondered if my years of study and my qualifications would go to waste; if I'd end up in a menial job I hated just to help pay the mortgage, because someone somewhere decided I wouldn't be qualified to do anything but raise a family. As it happened though, I didn't get to take too much time out at all. I dragged my third baby off to board meetings with me when he was six months old but soon realised that the corporate world wasn't that understanding when it came to mixing career and mothering. One day, I flew to Melbourne for a seminar and all eyebrows were raised as I sat there breastfeeding my ten month old. Gasp! I needed my baby with me as he was fully breastfed and it was clear that people weren't comfortable. What struck me as odd was that nobody seemed to even notice the guy with the seeing-eye dog. It was as if being a mother excluded me from fully participating in the corporate world.

I've been a solo business owner for four years and I've loved every minute of it. I am grateful to be avoiding the daily commute to the city, spending more quality time with my loved ones and avoiding job interviews and office politics. The thing is though, there are a lot of women out there who are struggling to meet their personal goals and needs. They are fed up with working as employees, or worse, feel trapped into full time employment to pay the mortgage, school fees etc. To me this is existing, not thriving. Women deserve better.

For women who have gone out on a limb and started their own enterprises, it's not necessarily been an easy ride either. A US study on successful women entrepreneurs showed that women-owned businesses are less likely to attract funding, less likely to be scaled into larger businesses and less likely to survive beyond two years. According to the 2013 Amex Open Forum study on *The State of Women-owned Businesses*, only 2% of women-owned businesses have broken through the one million dollar annual revenue barrier. Very few women are establishing high tech businesses, despite a boom in information and communication technology start-ups in the past few years. While women have experienced success in the corporate world in greater numbers than ever before, few are finding entrepreneurial success. However, the Amex Open Forum figures suggest this is changing. In a world that is becoming increasingly geared toward independent enterprise and technology, it's entrepreneurship that affords women the greatest autonomy and scope to leave their legacy.

> There is a global movement towards entrepreneurship, and women are forging their own paths forward in this new economic era.

As a business model, entrepreneurship is expansive. Rather than fighting over a limited pool of vendors and resources, creating something new means opening the door to new ventures and new income streams, new investments and new resources. As older business models fade away, the future of the global economy could well rest in the hands of the woman entrepreneur.

There is a global movement towards entrepreneurship, and women are forging their own paths forward in this new economic era. Despite ever-present gender discrimination, women have entered a new era of empowerment, and are redefining work, employment, the small business lifestyle and, indeed, success.

Society's reliance on the large corporate employer has been tainted by macro-economic events such as the great recession of 2008 to 2009, better known as the Global Financial Crisis (GFC). Unemployment continues to be a major problem in developed nations, and those at the pointy end of economic instability are looking, in greater numbers, towards having more control over their work life. Since the start of the GFC, there's been a growing trend towards low-growth, small scale ventures or micro businesses. For those working in these businesses, it means more perceived control and more flexibility. It means collaborating on a project-by-project basis with like-minded people who want to work together. The days where people were aligned in teams just for the sake of it are fading. Entrepreneurial thinking is starting to gain a foothold, even in large bureaucratic organisations and corporations. For governments this trend is troubling as they want to see businesses scale as well as higher employment figures, to prop up the economy. The worry is that the trend towards smaller enterprises will hamper economic stability in the long-term.

However, the more governments foster entrepreneurship, the more likely it will be that innovative thinkers will be encouraged to scale their ideas into businesses and their businesses into leading corporations. If corporate culture remains the same as it has been, driven by patriarchal and political models that do not consider their impact on the environment, on cultures and on families, governments and industry will find themselves fighting a losing battle. Something has to change in the way people work together, and this change always starts with those who choose to do things differently.

Perceptions and ideas about what success really means are shifting. For those who've been trodden on by ambitious, power-hungry colleagues or executives higher up the food chain, the corporate ladder may represent corruption, power, decadence, consumerism and multi-national abuse. The shift is subtle, but more people are seeking to shed the trappings of regular employment for a better existence and they are not afraid to be loud and proud about it.

Women in business have a unique opportunity to lead the way towards establishing a different paradigm; one that is more humane, one that encourages thoughtful leadership and one that acknowledges the complexities of modern family life. Women are no longer choosing between work in a corporate office and being home with the kids. These used to be perceived as the only viable choices for many women. Instead, they are choosing to found their own corporations, or do work they love from a home office or co-working space so they can better honour their personal commitments and professional goals. Women are no longer choosing to share only the expertise that's required of them in a corporate setting. Instead, they are choosing to value themselves and offer their expertise in a way that feels good to them. Women are no longer relying on corporate employers to provide job security. Instead, they are walking into banks, asking for loans and bravely setting up bricks and mortar shops, consultancies and services.

So how do you turn your ideas and life's purpose into a thriving enterprise that enables you to make the shift from employee to entrepreneur? That's what I'm sharing with you through this book.

My vision is that every woman staring down the barrel of life in the corporate workforce, a redundancy, career stagnation or a career change, knows she can take her destiny into her own hands. I want every woman who longs to turn her dream into a profitable enterprise to be empowered to succeed, on her terms, in her way. In essence, I want this book to instigate a movement that changes the stats on women-owned businesses.

Foreword

The definition of an entrepreneur is *a person who organises and manages any enterprise, especially a business, usually with considerable initiative and risk.*

In the past, the emphasis on the word 'risk' has held many people back from achieving success as an entrepreneur - particularly women.

Those times have changed.

The business world is changing, and changing fast. More women than ever before are choosing to take the leap to be entrepreneurs, foregoing the traditional trajectory of the 'one size fits all' climb up the corporate ladder. Instead, they are realising that they now have the opportunity to create successful businesses where they call the shots and are in control of their own destiny.

Women, by nature, are the perfect entrepreneurs. They have strong networking skills and excellent time-management and multi-tasking skills. In addition, many women have well-honed intuitive skills that are essential for keeping ahead of trends or understanding what their customer wants or needs.

All successful entrepreneurs need strong mentors; those who have forged the trail before them and are able to guide and teach the skills necessary to be a successful entrepreneur in the 21st Century.

Caroline McCullough is certainly a pioneer in the area of entrepreneurship. Not only has she managed to balance a number of businesses from her home-based office, and be the administrator of a very successful Facebook-based business group, but she also home-educates her three sons, two of whom are on the Autism spectrum.

The strategies Caroline used to create her balanced life are laid out in this easy to read, comprehensive book, which was written for all women who seek to create a viable, successful business.

Caroline does not sugarcoat the journey. In fact, she shares with the reader the good, the bad and the very challenging steps along the way.

In this brave new world of business we know that being a successful entrepreneur not only takes skills and desire, it also takes commitment and know-how. *Your Brilliant Un-Career* fills the gap, providing the strategies and tools to help you to create the successful business you desire.

Sally Thibault

Speaker, Author, Emotional Freedom Technique Practitioner

www.sallythibault.com.au

Contents

Introduction

If you have been longing to leap off the corporate ladder and get a life, or you're a corporate escapee, this book is for you.

Throughout this book I share my own personal (and often painful) journey, but interspersed with that is also a roadmap, complete with action steps, to help you break free from out-dated thinking about how to 'do business', and how to market your business. I want to challenge you to think well and truly outside the box when it comes to your capacity to quickly achieve the success, recognition and freedom you long for. If I can do it, you most certainly can!

Maybe you started up a micro business while your children were small, after being stuck on a corporate rung for years, or maybe you were made redundant and had to find other employment. Maybe you're playing out the corporate role you had in your business but you're not enjoying your work. Whatever path led you to this book, I want to encourage you to use this as a tool to hone in on your right path and work through the obstacles and barriers that may be standing in the way of your success. Each chapter addresses different issues that you may face along the way.

You don't need to read this book cover to cover. You can pick and choose the chapters that resonate with you. However, I recommend reading it from start to finish first, and then going back to the chapters that provide the most value for where you are at right now.

Using this book as a platform, be empowered to discover your profitable passion and set your own path to spectacular success!

Cheers to your brilliant un-career!

Chapter 1

Starting with your *why*

On being unemployable

If you were to take a snap shot of your life right now, would the picture show you doing something you truly love? Are you following a path that inspires you? Many people see work as functional, a necessity and a chore, but what if you could view work differently? What if you could follow a different path to the one that's been laid out for you? What if you were truly meant to do something else? It took me many years to realise that just because I *could* do something, it didn't mean I *should* do something. I first had to learn how to tune into my inner *why*.

It can take a long time to have that 'aha' moment, that moment when you realise your life's purpose was staring you in the face the whole time. My inner *why* had been screaming, stomping its feet and waving its arms, trying to get my attention for many years, in fact, since I was a little girl.

When I was nine, I was a free-spirited soul spending most of my days climbing trees, exploring the bush, running barefoot through creek beds and dreaming. After a close shave with the first of two Ash Wednesday bushfires, our family moved from our horse stud to the small town of Hahndorf in the Adelaide Hills, in South Australia. There was a small craft shop in the town and I loved wandering into the store after school each day to marvel at the handmade toys and dolls draped across the shop walls. I hadn't yet plucked up the courage to talk to the lady behind the shop counter, but she met me half way. After a few visits, Mrs Newell offered some felt for me to make something for myself. She was kind and generous with her felt leftovers, so I was in heaven.

I became a regular in her shop and her home, playing with her daughter and making felt bookmarks and toys that Mrs Newell could sell in her shop. What started out as a few cents here and there, quickly became a thriving enterprise that saw profits of up to $20 a week.

When I was 12, the second Ash Wednesday bushfire blackened the Adelaide Hills. While our home survived, not long after that our family moved to Queensland for a change of scene. I was heartbroken, leaving behind my wonderful little enterprise. As I grew older though, the outer world took over and I started to follow the same path as everyone else - going to school, watching copious amounts of TV and bitching about boys. I forgot the joy that came with making something new and lost my entrepreneurial spirit.

When I was 15, I was finally ready for my first 'real' job at Maccas. It was a lot of fun hanging out with the other kids in between shifts, eating crap and making prank calls from the staff dressing room. The only problem was that following the corporate mandate to put on a smile every day and serve highly processed food just didn't inspire me. That job was all about doing what you were told without question. When I did question things, it was made clear that my job was not to think, but to churn out orders as quickly as humanly possible. That should have been my first clue that working for a corporation wasn't for me. I was fired, and the kids at school made fun of me for not being able to hold down the first world's most menial job.

After that inglorious start, I had a string of jobs ranging from being a silver service waitress at a five star restaurant, to working as an executive at a large international corporation. I was hired and fired, quit some jobs and sabotaged others. I was bullied, harassed and labelled emotionally immature, self-centred and unemployable.

Some have said that my inability to conform was partly because I was labelled as having ADHD or being 'a bit Aspie', a term often used to describe people with Aspergers Syndrome, or what I call people with Aspersion tendencies. I actually prefer the term AHAIG = Accelerated, Hyper-Aware, and Incredibly Gifted. I don't like labels; they are limiting, but if it helps you understand me better, I'm happy to let these stick. As someone who is naturally pretty hyper, I was born with great capabilities; however most employers and teachers saw those capabilities as distractions, faux pas and fundamental flaws. Back in the 1970s and 80s, there was no support for 'different' children in schools. I learned to cope and learned the rules the hard way, through trial and error... and a hell of a lot of anxiety, frustration and tears.

I used to think that being unemployable was a curse, something to be ashamed of. I envied girls who seemed to be able to slot into any job with ease. I've realised since that I was never meant to work in a regular job. In school I was never very good at following rules and I didn't understand or have a great deal of respect for authority figures. Our teachers didn't exactly ooze 'respect me', and there was even one teacher who would regularly show up to class with the pungent smell of cheap whisky on his breath. I didn't consider myself to be a rebellious child, just a misunderstood one.

Perhaps, then, you'll understand why I simply did not fit into a corporate world where you had to do your time and work your way up the corporate ladder. Let's face it, I barely made it past the middle rung. So, eventually, after years of trying and failing to fit in, I quit trying to be employable and started working as a freelance marketing consultant. I had no idea that this way of working and collaborating would become the norm for a lot of people, not just misfits like me.

The irony is not lost on me that I went into corporate communications, given that interpersonal communication had always been a bit of a challenge, but I enjoyed writing and the adrenalin rush of working to event deadlines, so long as it meant I could work from home or not be tied to working at one place for very long.

The spark for my first startup: a year from hell!

My current entrepreneurial journey began with a pregnancy that went horribly wrong.

We'd had a year from hell. It was 2008, the year the GFC hit, and my husband had lost his father earlier in the year. It hit him hard and he started to spiral into serious depression. Shortly afterwards I found out I was pregnant, and for a while I wasn't sure if I should even share the news, but there was no hiding the morning sickness from my husband and our three boys. Despite the impact this news had on my husband, we both accepted what was to come and started making plans for the birth.

At about the eight week mark, I became gravely ill. Thinking it was just a bad case of gastro, I hurled my way through the next 48 hours. When I still wasn't feeling any better, I begged my husband to stay home from work. The problem was, he had an important meeting with his boss that day and he couldn't get out of it, so the two older kids were booked into after school care, and my four-year-old was positioned in front of the television.

Within an hour I started to feel massive surges of pain and my gut told me something was clearly very wrong. I called an ambulance, and eventually an emergency room ultrasound showed that my baby had positioned itself in my right fallopian tube. It had burst and I was bleeding internally so they had to rush to save my life.

After the surgery, collapsed lungs led to a nasty bout of pneumonia. The endless needles and tests, along with a partner who was quickly unravelling from the stress, and the loss of a much-wanted baby left me feeling overwhelmed. My mind toyed with the question, "What if I just slip away? That wouldn't be so bad, right?" At that very moment, though, a friendly midwife, who happened to be a friend of mine, walked into the room and said she'd be the one taking care of me that night.

It was then I realised that someone had my back, that no matter how bad things were, someone was watching over me. My thoughts strayed to my kids, who I had barely seen that week, and my heart ached.

In the long weeks afterward, my lungs and my broken heart slowly healed but my husband still struggled, and the GFC had stripped us of thousands of dollars in investments. There were days I stood at the grocery shop counter, nervous because I wasn't sure we had enough money in the bank to pay for our food. One day, I went to pay for petrol and my credit card was declined, so I had to endure the humiliation of filling out a form and leaving my licence at the counter while I went to find some cash. Life had to change. I knew that. I didn't want to wait any longer for my dreams to be handed to me.

When your life seems like it can't get any worse, you search for answers and comfort anywhere, and one place we ended up at was a small, local church. I went there to ask for prayer, and the preacher, a big-hearted man, prayed over us and blessed us with these words: "One day, you'll not only never have to worry about whether or not you have enough money to pay the grocery bill, you'll have enough to pay for the person behind you".

Mere words can spark hope, and what that preacher said that day was enough to keep me going and give me the small flame of belief and courage to think that, maybe one day, things might be different. It wasn't long before I started working towards my first startup business.

Finding my *why*

The idea sparked from a discussion with a friend in our mums' support group. At the time, I was a stay at home mum. We were talking about how wonderful it was to have a local support network during illness and after a baby was born. When I was sick, my friends delivered countless meals and helped us with chores. That support helped us through such a difficult time. I wanted all women to have access to support like that, but not every woman had the benefit of such an amazing local support network. At first, the idea was to be a collaborative one between a few of us, but in the end, I was the only one who was obsessed enough to follow through and make it happen. Thus my first business, Mumatopia, was born.

I had already started my training as a birth doula before the ectopic pregnancy, and it took me a good year to feel strong enough to continue with it. I was also waiting to have more money in our bank account to do things properly, but after listening to a radio interview with Australian entrepreneur and product licensing guru Justin Herald, I realised that I could start a business with virtually no startup budget. So, in February 2010, I arrived at the local business registration office with credit card in hand, and hoped my husband wouldn't notice $120 missing from our account. Our finances were still shaky but I knew that what I could offer women was invaluable and potentially life changing. I needed to take a leap of faith.

I have learned so much since then and the journey has changed me. It has made me stronger and more aware of my own strengths and weaknesses, as well as the triumphs and pitfalls of running a business. At times it's been devastating and damned hard, but that is the nature of running your own business. The road won't always be straight but it will be worth it!

In the years since then, I have owned and co-owned four businesses. I still occasionally attend births, but have moved on to create a primary business that enables me to empower women (and quite a few men) on a much larger scale. Being an entrepreneur has stretched me and given me amazing gifts, not to mention an income, but the journey has been fuelled by an overarching *why*.

My *why* is that I want to change the stats on women-owned businesses. Empowering women has always been the driving force behind my work, and no doubt it will continue to be, long into the future. Aside from raising three happy boys, helping entrepreneurs, especially women entrepreneurs, understand that pursuing their dreams is valuable, that they are valuable and to realise their potential is what gets me out of bed in the morning.

Lessons learned from little people with big passions

Another thing that helped me to kick-start my entrepreneurial un-career has been my parenting journey. As a parent, I see my kids struggle with some of the same issues that baffled me as a child. My eldest child has Asperger's Syndrome. He's incredibly focused and knowledgeable about the topics he's passionate about. He is literal and likes people to be reliable and fair. My number two son is autistic and struggles with an auditory processing and speech disorder. Every day I see him reach out and try to relate to others. I can see he so badly wants to connect, but needs a bit more practice, and his language barrier often gets in the way. My youngest is a feisty young man with an artistic temperament, who loves to create incredibly complex games, sing, dance and talk...constantly.

I don't know if my children will grow up to be entrepreneurs, but they will grow up to follow their passions because that's what they're doing now, and they've been born into an exciting world where opportunity is everywhere and people find fortune and fame with the click of a mouse. This is the world they relate to so easily, while the grownups around them are just trying to keep pace with technological change.

As my kids are home-educated, every day, I watch them pursue what interests them most, whether it be building imaginary worlds on Minecraft or filming sci-fi movies in the backyard. What they've taught me is that by following your heart and doing what you love, you can make your greatest contribution to the world. Little did I know that this unorthodox life we'd begun would also open the door for me to follow my own dreams, but that's exactly what has happened. In the midst of mothering and home educating, I started up my own small business and thus began my brilliant un-career. I say un-career because it often doesn't look like a career and sometimes it doesn't resemble work, but I do provide services and information that people value, so I guess you could class it as work, if you really wanted to. I prefer to think of what I do as going on an entrepreneurial adventure. When you love what you do, it doesn't seem like work at all.

> I say un-career because it often doesn't look like a career and sometimes it doesn't resemble work.

The difference between a career and an adventure is this: Pursuing a career means doing one thing for a long time, really well. You may gradually work your way towards more prestige, profits and power, or you may remain in the same position for years on end, chipping away at the endless, seemingly important tasks that are thrown your way. An adventure is more about the journey than it is about the destination. You may change course halfway through, but that's okay. It's your journey. You get to decide what path you follow. An adventure is not about power or prestige, it is about freedom to be who you are and leave your legacy in a way that you choose. You don't always know what the outcome will be, and that's thrilling.

What's your motivation for starting up?

There has never been a better time to start up a business. Virtually anyone, anywhere, can start an internet business and for many people, especially mum entrepreneurs (mumpreneurs) with young children, this is an appealing prospect.

Your *why* is your reason for starting up in the first place, your intrinsic motivation. Your *why* fuels your mission and ensures you stay focused, even when the road to business success is a tad bumpy.

While you are thinking about your *why,* consider that a Kauffman Foundation study found five primary financial and psychological factors common amongst both men and women founders:

1. The desire to build wealth

2. The wish to capitalise on business ideas they had

3. The appeal of startup culture

4. A long-standing desire to own their own company

5. Working for someone else did not appeal to them

Interestingly though, the study found that women were more likely than men to consider joining a startup if another founder encouraged them. Is this because women don't think of starting up their own business as a viable prospect, or is it because they lack confidence in themselves? It could be either. I know that founding a business wasn't something I felt confident about to begin with, but with encouragement from my peers, I gained confidence over time. I wish I could say that confidence was just oozing out of me, but it really did take a kick up the butt from some colleagues to get moving. I needed to see what they saw in me—my awesomeness! If you're not seeing your awesomeness yet, my goal is that you will by the time you finish this book.

While both men and women identified the above five factors as important, women were more likely to cite workplace conditions, the prospect of improved income and an unhappiness with working for someone else as reasons to quit the corporate ladder.

These factors are certainly incentives to found a business, but are any of them enough to keep you going through the ups and downs of owning and running your own venture? Let's explore this for a minute. Can you pinpoint your underlying desires, dreams, goals and motivations?

Are those desires, dreams, goals and motivations genuine interests and obsessions, or are they dictated by your life circumstances? A redundancy, an illness, debts, a marriage breakdown, a death in the family, your income, a disability etc., can push you towards a decision you may not have made otherwise. Circumstances can shape your *why*, but if they are the only determining factor, you may find that you are so stressed about the outcome that you don't enjoy the journey and you certainly won't be following your dream. You are more likely to succeed if your motivations, goals, dreams and desires come from within rather than from your outward circumstances.

There are many examples of people who beat the odds and went from dire circumstances to phenomenal success, but in most of these stories, it wasn't their circumstances that lead them to make something of themselves. Singer songwriter Jewel famously lived in her car before getting her big break. J. K. Rowling was a struggling single mum when she wrote Harry Potter. The bottom line is that your circumstances do not define your path, even if they provide some inspiration and motivation to get moving on establishing your brilliant un-career.

Unmet needs can also inspire your *why*. If an unmet need leads you to thinking of something truly innovative, then that's awesome. However, if it just leads you to pounce on any project that remotely relates then that could cause problems for you down the line.

Really, your *why* is whatever you are most passionate about. It is what gets you leaping out of bed in the morning and what drives you internally. Get the heart of what really fuels your spirit and you've found your *why*. Not every *why* can and should be a business venture, but every business venture should be fuelled by a rock solid *why*. The next step is to turn that business *why* into an enterprise.

> Not every *why* can and should be a business venture, but every business venture should be fuelled by a rock solid *why*.

Questions for you to ponder:

- If you have an interest you'd like to turn into a profitable venture, do you feel ready to explore it?

- Perhaps you have a book in you, or you can see yourself running your own workshops in cities around the world. What dream do you have that seems far off but could be brought closer with a strategy in place?

- Is there a story you are telling yourself that could be holding you back from reaching your greatest potential?

These are all big questions, but ones you'll want to answer if you want to get to the heart of your *why*. If you have a profound understanding of what's fuelling your *why*, when the insecurities crop up, you can recognise them, acknowledge them and gain clarity to keep you going through business building's harder moments.

Entrepreneurs who value making a difference in the world know their *why*. Most entrepreneurs don't go down the path of establishing a new venture without a serious amount of passion for their projects. Without passion driving a startup, survival during the tough times is difficult. Know your *why* and it will be your guide on the entrepreneurial journey, and if your *why* is a little thin, perhaps you need to take a bit more time to think about what it is that truly gets you leaping out of bed in the morning before founding your own business or changing direction in your current business.

Un-Career Story

Dana left behind the corporate world to establish her coaching business.

Dana's Story

I truly had a great experience over my first few years in the corporate world, with many opportunities for growth, great leadership and a supportive community. Then the economic downturn hit. While I was lucky and survived not one, not two, not three, but four rounds of layoffs, it was heartbreaking to see my talented colleagues be let go. Women just like me who had given their heart and soul to the company. It started me thinking that if I were going to give my all to something, I wanted it to be something no one could take away from me. But I wasn't quite ready to make a big move yet. I was in the middle of my second pregnancy and in the midst of the difficult economic climate, so I stayed where I was.

Fast forward to the Summer of 2011 and my life forever changed. My father, who had been fighting a brave and fearless battle with lung cancer, passed away. I was fortunate to be able to spend a good deal of time with him in those final weeks, and during that time, I did a lot of thinking about where my life was going and what my purpose was. I realised that while I was good at what I did, and made a good living at it, it wasn't what I was put on the earth to do. I had a background in psychology and had always been interested in coaching, so I started to research the industry and enrolled in coach training. I was still working full time while I studied and took on private clients, so was able to make a gradual transition.

What inspires me to keep going is staying focused on my mission - to empower others to do what they love and live abundant lives while being of great service in the world. When I have a tough day, I remember - it's not about me, it's about my mission. And I just keep going.

The most effective marketing methods for my business and personality are networking, building strategic partnerships, speaking, providing valuable, free content to my audience and social media.

Time management was my greatest challenge, but I knew I needed to master this in order to achieve my goals. I now teach others exactly what I had to learn for myself in this area.

There are four strategies that help the most with juggling my family, personal commitments and my business:

1. Ruthless prioritisation - being crystal clear on my top priorities and focusing my energy there; letting the small stuff go

2. Being diligent with planning - knowing exactly what I need to focus on each day in order to achieve my larger objectives

3. Getting help - house cleaning, child care, virtual assistant, web support, etc.

4. Committing to extreme self care - I can only be as effective as my personal energy level allows

If you're thinking about starting your own business, get clear on your big *why* and remain laser-focused on it. Have a solid plan and understand your numbers. Don't reinvent the wheel. Find others who have done what you've done and learn from or model them. Get comfortable with self-promotion. Shift your mindset from 'marketing and sales' to 'sharing and inviting'. Remember, done is better than perfect! Get out there, take action and tweak as needed.

Dana D'Orsi from Dana D'Orsi International, danadorsi.com, lives in Coventry, Rhode Island, USA.

Pitfalls of a shaky *why*

Without a solid *why* in place, your resolve may falter and your dream may come to an abrupt end. Everybody's *why* is completely unique, but there are some *why*s that have been proven to cause a business to fail. Below are some of the most common ones.

You want to make easy money

Wanting to make easy money is absolutely normal. You don't start a business with a goal to make no money, and you don't set out to slave away for hours on end. A healthy passive income would be great, but understand that the idea of making easy money is a bit of a myth. You will need to plan, be strategic and work hard (at least initially) to get the easy money flowing.

However, if making easy money is the only thing driving your business idea, then the entrepreneurial life is probably not for you. Establishing a business is not easy. It takes hard work and tenacity. Unless you have a 'never say die' attitude, one day something will happen that will send your house of cards toppling down. If money is your *why*, what is going to sustain you when times are tough?

Action Step

Jot down some ideas for passive income
and then start to do some research on what
it takes to get these income streams going.
What are some common pitfalls? What are some
of the benefits?

You want to capitalise on a trend

It happens a lot in the business world. Someone invents the latest, coolest, must-have item and within days there are imitations aplenty. This isn't just happening with mass-produced products. It's happening with whole business concepts and movements. An interesting case study is the Etsy phenomenon. Etsy, an online ecommerce community for handmade crafters and people who sell vintage items, has grown into a multi-million-dollar enterprise. Their *why* was primarily driven by an environmental and anti-consumerist ideal. It is this *why* that has spawned the incredibly diverse handmade craft industry flourishing on Etsy.

However, since Facebook Business Pages were launched, many home-based craft businesses have hung out their shingles, not because they wanted to change the world, produce more environmentally conscious products or encourage people to re-purpose old things, but because they wanted to make easy money and capitalise on a trend.

While there are many talented artists and creative entrepreneurs in the online space who are driven by more than economic factors, there are also many people selling poor quality craft items and, dare I say it, mass-produced handmade items. After all, if you are producing items in such large numbers that you could be working on a factory floor, it's mass-produced. I used to make handmade décor and accessories when I first founded Mumatopia. I loved doing it and I even made some money out of it. But in the end, I stopped creating because it felt like I was working on an assembly line, and it just stopped being fun. I also came to the realisation that I wasn't effectively leveraging my expertise.

It's okay to put your take on things, to take inspiration from a trend and go with it. That's called progress. A really great example of this is the plethora of online business coaches in the marketplace. All of them have capitalised on a trend, but for some, the really good ones, they've also been motivated by something other than making a quick, easy buck. If you feel inspired by a current trend, really think about what's motivating you and analyse the longevity and authenticity of your business proposition. Is this trend likely to continue into the long term? Is it going to inspire a whole wave of new innovations?

Action Step

Are you able to meet a gap in the market that no one else is seeing? Are you able to put your own spin on a trend and make it entirely your own?

You want to be famous for something (anything will do)

The Law of Attraction movement has sprung to life with almost religious fever from the book *The Secret.* The movement has promoted the idea that you can achieve what you want and manifest your wildest dreams, that you are perfection, and if anyone disagrees they are simply out of alignment with you.

One of the big sidelines that has come out of this movement is the wealth creation industry. Fame and fortune hunters are everywhere! There is a whole industry devoted to training people how to become famous, and how to leverage that celebrity to create wealth. The problem is that many are not driven by anything more than the idea of living the lifestyle of the rich and famous. If your vision of luxury and wealth is your *why,* then your *why* lacks substance, ideals, or true passion, and the chances of actually attaining that goal are slim to none. If you don't have something substantial motivating you to get up and move forward, you may give up when you hit the inevitable roadblocks on the rocky road to success.

The most successful famous people I know of are also the most humble and most unassuming souls on this planet. Fame can have its downsides such as a loss of privacy and a feeling like your life is not your own (not that I would know, because I'm not exactly famous). Being famous and rich could be lots of fun, and you definitely shouldn't rule it out or sabotage your efforts in a bid to avoid it, but take some time to think through how it might affect you and those you love in the long-term.

Positive *whys*

Now that we've had a look at some of the *whys* that can lead to small business failure, how about we check out some of the *whys* that can sustain you on the winding road to business success.

You believe in a cause

Many enterprise ideas are kick-started from life experience and a belief in a cause. If you truly believe in something, you will naturally be more committed to seeing it through when the road gets rough. With a great team in place to provide balance and advocacy, and a solid business structure to ensure your plans can come to fruition, conviction can be the fuel that keeps the fires burning through the hard times. A good leader will recognise the need to take advice before diving in, but will also be energised by her belief and have the perseverance to see something through that others may not.

> People who are motivated to make a difference have the bigger picture in mind when they start a business.

You want to make a difference

Even if you don't have a cause you believe in, you may want to do something meaningful to make a positive dent in the tapestry of the world. Many service professionals are motivated by the desire to do something to make an impact on the world. The trick is to figure out what the thing is that you can do and should do to make the impact you'd like to. If you're motivated to make a difference, the good news is that you'll be able to draw upon this whenever you make decisions about the direction of your business. Is the direction you are considering in alignment with your greater goal? If it isn't, you can alter course to stay on track. People who are motivated to make a difference have the bigger picture in mind when they start a business. Having a great team around them will help turn this motivation into reality.

Un-Career Story

Krishna's story highlights how she started a business fuelled by a passion to make a difference.

Krishna's story

My husband and I have worked for ourselves for the past ten years. Deane is a massage therapist who recently moved into a practice, and I operate my marketing consultancy and training business from home.

What led me to leave the corporate world was making the transition from a media/advertising career into the health industry. I was a fitness instructor, and worked in health promotion. A move interstate lead to the beginning of a health products ecommerce site. This became a marketing consultancy when I saw a big gap in the marketing training and services available for heart-centered entrepreneurs.

I light up when I talk about my work. It's my greatest indicator that I'm meant to be doing this! It's my contribution to the greater good as I am able to to work with people who have important missions and purposes to make a difference.

What I find challenging is my close family's attitude towards my endeavours. I look to others in my network for inspiration instead.

I primarily market my business through networking - a combination of on and offline networking brings my leads in. I get direct referrals through personal contacts and Facebook. Most of my marketing is social, and fun to do, which is something I teach to others through my 'Passionate Marketing' program.

I work predominantly when my children are at school, and physically switch off at 3pm. I'll often work in the evening after they are in bed if I have projects that involve more time. If I have workshops or all day events, these are scheduled in advance with my husband's diary, so he can allocate time for the children. It works for us!

If I had any advice to give others looking to go down the same pathway, I would say: define your non-negotiables. It's no good saying you are leaving the corporate life to be with your family, and then leaving no time for them! Don't undersell yourself or your value.

Be realistic about the time it will take to generate momentum. Make sure you are financially stable, and if there is a period of transition, that's okay. Get help! Don't do it alone or allow yourself to be isolated. Become part of a mastermind group with others for support. Network, and embrace social media.

Krishna Everson from Healthy Marketing, krishnaeversonmarketing.com.au, is from The Sunshine Coast, Queensland, Australia.

You want to pioneer change

Some of the best inventions and trends have started from someone seeing a need that nobody else saw. Facebook is a classic example of this, and look at the difference this technological innovation has made to the world. Pioneers are passionate and they want to make a difference. They want to change the way we live in fundamental ways to make people's lives easier, more fulfilling and more dynamic. For instance, pioneers making innovations in medical technology have allowed people to live happier, healthier lives. Pioneers are resilient because they know that many people will see them as lone nuts before they see them as leaders and innovators. Pioneers are forward thinking and always have one foot in the future. This can be a real asset on the path to success. Pioneers do need to be able to straddle the present along with the future though, or they risk moving forward too quickly and forgetting about the fine print that underlies sustainability.

Un-Career Story

Jan moved from being led by her circumstances to being led by her *why*.

Jan's Story

I am a widow, the mother of a beautiful daughter who lives in Darwin, and the grandmother of two boys. I have faced a lot of adversity in life with losing my partner to Alzheimer's Dementia, faced my own mortality dealing with cancer and now, eight years down the track, I am still healthy and moving forward.

I had set an intention when I was 25 that I would retire and live my life at 55. I was not aware at the time how this would happen. Just 17 days after my 55th birthday, I was made redundant. I had worked in the public service arena for 30 years and although I had time away, I always found my way back into this corporate world. I can now see that I stayed there because it was safe. It suited me, or so I thought. When I became aware of the entrepreneurial world I realised I was not in flow, nor was I doing the job that was best suited to me. I did it because I thought it was part of providing a service... oh how wrong I was.

Being made redundant threw me into entrepreneurship and I am so grateful now for the strength this has given me to move forward and create my business.

I am in startup mode and loving the new challenges. I've written a book, *The Well Used Keys,* which aims to inspire teenagers and young adults to be the very best they can be, and to take the action needed to gain the success they want for their life. My second book is about the success of my athletic endeavours and how I saw in my mind's eye the race before it was even run. This will be accompanied by programs to help young people create their own success step by step.

The biggest challenges of being a startup business have been cash flow, learning new aspects of business I have never encountered before, and staying in flow while doing everything myself. Of course in the early stages I haven't been able to pay a team to support me. I have engaged with some business mentors though, and they are guiding me as I grow.

What keeps me inspired is knowing I can be a huge influence to my two grandsons and being able to help them see the world through another set of eyes. I know I can leave a legacy that will be held for future generations to learn and grow, just as I have learned from my past teachers, such as Napoleon Hill, Maxwell Maltz and current teachers John Assaraf, John De Martini and Bob Proctor.

Being now just 12 months on from redundancy I can see how I am so much happier and find I do not have to juggle anywhere near as much as I had to in the corporate world. Also, being a mature age entrepreneur, my family is self-sufficient, so the journey has been mostly carefree and easy. The best tip I could share with other corporate escapees is to be true to yourself and really follow your heart. Know that when it does not feel good, you are off track, need to pull back and realign to what your heart wants the most. Then you can get back into the river of flow and be guided by this.

If you are thinking about leaping from the corporate ladder, just do it!! If you have a clear passion and you're working on something that is inspiring to you outside of the corporate world, then follow your heart and make the adjustments.

Jan Muir from I Believe I Achieve lives on
The Gold Coast, Queensland, Australia.
facebook.com/AuthorJanMuir

⭐ Action Step

List five *whys* underlying your business dream. Are they intrinsic (internally motivated) or extrinsic (externally motivated).

What are some of the strengths and weaknesses of these core *whys*?

Bonus: Download bonus resources that dig deeper into this topic. For this chapter, I interviewed author and entrepreneur Shar Moore on finding your purpose. There's also a free Finding Your *Why* worksheet and a printable affirmation to inspire you to take action now. To access these bonus resources, simply sign up here: bit.ly/uncareerresources

Chapter 2

Entrepreneurship in the information economy

The information economy has dramatically changed the entrepreneurial landscape over the past ten years or so. Entrepreneurship used to be the domain of product marketers, but now the tide is turning and there are limitless possibilities to extend your reach and expand your ideas through developing information products and programs. This trend was foreseen as early as 1977, when the term 'information economy' was coined in a US government report on the topic. Never before has it been so easy to run a professional development program, a conference or a workshop from the comfort of your own home office or co-working space.

When I first started a business, creating an information-based enterprise was far from my agenda. All I wanted to do, initially, was to serve women in the local community as a birth and postnatal doula. After a year or so, I realised I'd need to supplement my income with something else. My problem wasn't in attracting clients. Mumatopia's branding was doing the job, and I was using every tool available to me. The biggest problem was that I was exchanging money for time. As a doula who was also a home-educating mumma to three growing boys, I could only attend one birth every six weeks and that meant being on call every month a woman was due to give birth. Being on call for weeks on end and disappearing at a moment's notice was hard on the family, so I made the decision to only attend occasional births until my kids were older and more independent.

With the time this opened up for me, I felt driven to create an information-based business in part to support the international birth reform movement, a group of health practitioners and other individuals and organisations who are passionate about making a significant difference to the lives of others through improving childbirth. I now am focused on my marketing consultancy. I am blessed to be able to work with a variety of clients, including midwives, childbirth experts, allied health practitioners and doulas, as a marketing mentor.

Establishing an information-based business has transformed my life. I now do most of my work from home and when I run group training programs, they only take up a couple of hours in my day. While I spend a considerable amount of time developing the content for my programs and workshops, I am at the point now where I can just tweak the information every time I run a new program iteration. I've also been able to create products from the material in my programs (you're reading one right now!). The benefit of running group programs and creating products is that I am no longer exchanging money for time, but money for expertise.

There are countless ways in which entrepreneurs are thriving in the information economy. Here are a few examples to inspire you to use your expertise to its greatest potential.

Blogs and podcasts

When I was at high school, a newspaper journalist in a checkered suit visited our class to tell us about journalism, and I was hooked. Back then, of course, it was extremely difficult to get an internship with a newspaper or even a PR or advertising firm. When I was looking for my first graduate job, I collected about 80 rejection letters. My first graduate position ended up being in marketing administration, which eventually led to bigger and better opportunities. These days, you don't have to rely on the media industry to provide writing and reporting opportunities. If you feel compelled to share something with the world and can write or speak well, you can take your publishing destiny into your own hands through a blog, vlog or podcast.

A blog is an online repository of self-published articles, a podcast is like a radio or TV show, only you record it and then upload it to iTunes or another podcasting platform for distribution. A vlog is similar to a podcast only it is in video format only. You don't need to rely on getting past gatekeepers to follow your dream. You can start blogging about something you're keenly interested in right now. There are literally thousands of quality resources available online about how to blog and podcast. If this is something you want to do, all you need is to decide to get started.

Making money from blogging and podcasting

It can take time to build your blog or podcast to the point where you can attract advertising income, sponsorship or publishing deals. Successful overnight blogs are rare indeed. However, if you use these tools as part of an overall strategy, and you're hitting the spot with your readers, eventually you will get there. Keep your focus on being genuine, telling your story and helping others through what you share.

Action Step

What are you so interested in you feel compelled to share it with the world? What expertise can you share through a blog or podcast?

Mobile apps and games

App and game development is all the rage and this market is only going to grow, especially with new technology coming out that further integrates technology with our lives. If you want to learn how to develop apps, the information is readily available on the internet. If you want to learn how to code, there are numerous courses and training programs available. Technology is a growth area in which women are yet to showcase their prowess on a grand scale. If coding isn't your thing, you can outsource the coding to a freelancer on elance.com or another freelancing website.

Action Step

If you could develop an app, what would it be for?

Business coaching

Attending a course at university can be incredibly expensive, so when you have a particular professional development need, attending a virtual class with a business coach can be an economical solution. These days, business coaches abound and women are well and truly leading the charge in the industry. Business coaching enables you to make a living out of sharing your expertise and leveraging your skills. There is a science to successful business coaching, but there are plenty of coaching experts available to guide you as you develop your own programs and products. I really enjoy working with my coaching clients and it is rewarding to be able to make a difference to other businesses through sharing my expertise.

Life coaching

If you love to work with others to transform their personal lives, life coaching may be your cup of tea. Before business coaching really took off, life coaching was in its heyday. People looking to establish a more fulfilling life were turning to certified life coaches to mentor them on the path to enlightenment, fulfilment and self-actualisation. Life coaches present an alternative to seeing a psychologist, but it is their active involvement and guidance that sets them apart from psychologists and psychiatrists. However, they don't just work with troubled souls. Life coaches work with people who are working through less traumatic personal issues that may get in the way of their success and freedom. Life coaches often come out of medicine, natural medicine, nutrition, social work, psychology, human resources and other service-based positions.

Passive income streams

You can create passive income in a number of ways and the information economy presents new opportunities that did not exist ten or 20 years ago. These are three of the most common strategies used in the online space:

Website advertising

Every other day I receive an email asking if my website accepts advertising or if I do sponsored blog posts. Blog ads can be a great way to build passive revenue, but if you're not careful, they can also do a lot of damage to your reputation. So, it's important to assess whether or not ads are suitable for your site and what kind of ads would be the most appropriate.

When considering an advertiser, ask yourself:

- Does this build my credibility?

- Does this appeal to my ideal clients and customers?

So, when are ads appropriate?

On business blogs, ads can be appropriate and even credibility-building when they are carefully selected and fit with your target audience.

Be judicious with tools such as Ad Choices and Google Ads, as you cannot completely control what appears on your website. If you have a website that appeals to a broad audience, anything-goes-style ads may really work for you. However, if you are aiming to draw a specific target audience to your blog, raise awareness about important issues or if you work as a consultant or service provider of some kind, your website would be better served by more carefully targeted advertising. Steer clear of ads you can't control and work with advertisers that you have a relationship with.

If you want to earn some passive income from advertising revenue, bear in mind that the ads should fit the audience. If your target market is savvy, informed women and you have teen ads all over your blog, you'll lose out on exposure. Keep in mind also that if people are drawn to your blog primarily for must-have information, cluttering your blog with ads may diminish your perceived authority and credibility.

Action Step

Based on the above information, what kinds of advertising would work for your website or blog?

Affiliate marketing

When you work for yourself, it makes sense to look for ways you can make money in your sleep. One of the easiest ways you can make some extra passive income is to sign up to affiliate programs where you receive a commission for each sale made on the advertised products. Businesses large and small use affiliate or referral programs to market their programs, products and events. It is one of the most common forms of marketing used for online businesses.

If you are keen to explore using affiliate programs to grow your income, first identify if affiliate programs are right for your business, then explore what opportunities are a good fit for your business and how to go about promoting the programs you align yourself with. These ten tips will help you with that process:

1. Choose businesses that are in alignment with your business and branding. If you promote products, events or services that are out of alignment with your branding, you will be unlikely to attract affiliate income. It may sound obvious but there are lots of websites out there with poorly matched advertising. Ask yourself: Does this complement my branding? Does it align with my values? If you answer 'no' to either of these questions, keep a wide berth.

2. Ask how the product could help your niche market. Align yourself with brands that can offer something valuable to your ideal customers and clients. If you can offer extra value to your leads and customers through the affiliates you are aligned with, it will have a flow-on effect to your business. Ask yourself whether people will thank you for introducing them to this business.

3. Make a spreadsheet or use a service like Lastpass.com or Roboform.com to help you keep track of your affiliate programs, logins and other information. Once you sign up for a few programs, it can be

really difficult to keep track of all the details. If you have to make changes to your affiliate profiles, it takes a lot less time if you are organised.

4. Follow your affiliate businesses using the list functions on social media and have special inboxes set up on your email to keep track of new programs. The affiliate programs I have signed up for are all with businesses I've been following for a while. However, occasionally you may come across a new one you'd like to try out via an organic web search or via word of mouth.

5. Ask yourself how much time you'll need to spend on each affiliate program you are considering in order to receive a worthwhile return on your investment. Many programs offer significant percentages but some do not. As a guide, anywhere between 40 to 60% is worth putting more effort into.

6. Look for programs that give you all the information you need, such as links, ads etc. Some are great at doing this, some are not. Affiliates that hold your hand through the process make it easy for you to promote their events and products. Use this tip if you are looking at running affiliate programs or looking to sign up to some. Not every affiliate program needs a lot of promotion but if the goal is to earn passive income, you want to make your life easier, not more complicated and stressful.

7. Disclose your interest when you promote. You can state this openly on your website or put it into your post as part of a testimony. It's really important to be up-front with your visitors, followers and customers. State, for the record, that you are proud to align yourself with the product or event.

8. Use your own words and speak from the heart, but take guidance from pro-formas. Although many affiliates want to put words in your mouth, it is always a good idea to personalise emails, tweets and Facebook posts. People can smell inauthenticity a mile off. If they've seen the same post from a number of affiliates, they'll be less likely to buy via your affiliate link.

9. Be consistent and regular, but don't over-promote. When you do promote an event or product, be sure to promote it at different times of the day and in different ways.

10. Commit to fully promoting the affiliate program. If you do things half-heartedly you won't reap the rewards. Use social media to get the word out as you would your own campaigns. Placing one ad on your blog may

reap some rewards, but drawing attention to it and stating why it is helpful to your ideal clients and customers is even better.

Action Step

Take ten minutes to make a list of business experts or service providers you are considering affiliating with. Go to their websites and search for an affiliate page. If they have one, check out the terms and conditions and see if they are a good fit for you.

Information products

Creating information products that showcase your knowledge and expertise can be a terrific complement to your online training programs, your blog and your business. Information products can come in the form of reports, research findings, how-to guides, ecourses, ebooks, webinars, worksheets and more.

Information products are great as subscriber incentives, as bonuses at events or program launches, and as stand-alone products to sell on your website.

A lot of online marketers look to information products as the answer to creating passive income. However, there are so many products, books and ecourses available these days, it takes a lot of not-so-passive marketing to really get your products out there and selling well. The sage advice given to me by business coach Annemarie Cross was to develop a range of information products, but not to rely on them solely for your income. Great advice!

Action Step

What kinds of information products could you develop right now to make passive income for your business?

Un-Career Story

Meredith shows how developing an information product helped her establish a viable business without compromising time with her children.

Meredith's Story

We moved from Washington DC to Albuquerque, NM to be closer to our West Coast family. My daughter was three, so I decided I could have my cake and eat it too by starting my own business and working around my daughter's hours, rather than working full time in a place with notoriously low salaries.

My company gives women the tools they need to create a business based on their passions and talents. I have used every shopping cart, CRM and email system out there, so I know what works. I help match people with the right systems for them, and can custom-make systems when required. I have a website, use social media and write a newsletter, but most of my business comes from personal referrals.

I learned that if your business is educational in nature, figure out what intellectual property you want to share, then find some people to teach what you don't know. As your business grows and makes money, you can start making arrangements to exit if that's what you want. You don't need to do everything at once; Rome wasn't built in a day...

Time management and task management are my biggest challenges. It is hard to resist spending all your time working, and sometimes it's hard to get all your work done when life intervenes. You need to really think about *why* you are in business. If it is to spend more time with your family, then make sure you do that! It is too easy to get caught up in work and then forget why you are working so hard in the first place.

I look at my clients who make a good living sharing their passions and dreams with others and that inspires me to keep going. I know that they would not have the lives they have without my help. I am also inspired to be a role model for my daughter; to show her that you can work on your own terms.

Meredith Eisenberg from Paycheck to Passion,
paychecktopassion.com, lives in Albuquerque, New Mexico, USA.

Bonus: Download bonus resources that dig deeper into this topic. For this chapter, I interviewed Bec Derrington founder of Sourcebottle.com on entrepreneurship in the information economy. There's also a free Tech Action Plan template and a printable affirmation to inspire you to take action now. To access these bonus resources, simply sign up here: bit.ly/uncareerresources

Chapter 3

Understanding and
overcoming barriers
to business success

Being in business for yourself is one of the most intense personal development programs out there. You will have ups and downs, you will gain a lot of personal insight, and you will grow and change in the process. I have never learned so much or grown so much in such a short time frame as when I started a business.

There are always things we wish we knew 'back then', those things that might prevent us from making hideous mistakes, but in life, mistakes are sometimes necessary. That said, it helps to have an idea of some of the potholes, roadblocks and meandering paths along the way. If you can avoid some of the common business mistakes that many fresh-faced business newbies make, you'll be able to fail fast then pivot on your heels so you can move forward and achieve the success you deserve. Below I share ten of the most common barriers to business growth, as well as some possible solutions.

1. Gaping holes in your marketing system

If you're facing the prospect of shutting down due to poor sales, ask yourself: Have I done everything I can to make this a success? Where are the gaps in my online and offline marketing?

There could be any number of things holding you back from achieving your potential as a business owner. These could be as simple as:

- Blurry product photos or product photos that don't stand out

- Overly wordy product descriptions, and 'About' sections

- Over-posting boring content on social media

- Incomplete social media profiles

- Self-promoting on social media instead of building relationships

- Inconsistent branding, or branding that simply doesn't reflect the quality of what you do

- Sales information that doesn't show the true value of what you offer

- Spamming people with email newsletters they never subscribed to

I could go on, but you get the picture.

Sadly, I've seen many micro businesses give up and blame a lack of visibility for poor sales. However, the smallest changes could make a difference. Try some of these strategies:

- Reviewing your Facebook insights to get clues about post popularity and timing of posts

- Hiring a professional product photographer to take more appealing photos of you, your products and service delivery. If you can't afford to hire one, can you barter?

- Engaging a professional website designer to give your website an overhaul. There are many website designers who work from home. You can even find them on Elance.com or oDesk.com

- Ensuring your social media is linked to your offline marketing efforts. You can generate more fans for your business page through fans who've already engaged with you in real life

- Using the free posters from Facebook at markets and in stores to showcase that your business is on Facebook

It's heartbreaking to see businesses shut up shop when they could have made changes to turn their businesses around.

⭐ Action Step

Make a list of everything you are doing in your marketing right now, or plan to do if you have yet to make the leap. Save this list for later. You'll need it in Chapter Seven, where we go into detail about how to find and address the gaps in your marketing and how to set up a robust marketing system.

2. Burn out because you've tried to do everything yourself

Many entrepreneurs take pride in being shoestring marketers and learning how to do things themselves. When you first start a business, you may not have the budget to outsource work to others. However, if you spend too much time working in your business, you will not have as much time to work on your business and grow it.

Below are some common areas where solo business owners may need a helping hand:

Childcare

If you have small children at home, it may be tempting to think you can work around nap times. This may be the case for a period. However, most women solo business owners find they need to organise childcare at some point in the journey. Childcare options include babysitters, nannies, au pairs, family daycare, kindergarten and childcare centres.

Cleaning

I've had cleaners on and off and I find that when I do have one, I'm more able to focus on my work. When our family has been cleaner-less, I've noticed a difference in how I've felt. Even if you have a cleaner come in for a spring clean once a quarter, it will help you stay focused and re-energise you. Remember that cleaning should not be your sole responsibility. Get every member of the family involved from an early age to ease the burden. Make it clear to your partner, if you have one, that you need them to contribute to household chores. If having a cleaner is not within your budget, there may be some creative ways to make it happen, such as forming a cleaning co-op with other business owners.

Cooking

I used to love baking and creating gourmet family meals but sadly, running my own business has meant that I rarely get to do either these days. Nowadays, preparing the family meals feels like a chore rather than a creative activity. Fortunately my kids love to bake and often cajole me to help them make chocolate chip cookies or cupcakes, but I often struggle with the day to day stuff and sometimes forget to eat altogether. If you're the same, here are a couple of ideas you may find helpful:

- Host baking days where you get together with friends and make a whole heap of food so you don't have to cook for a week

- Hire a personal chef. If your budget allows, getting a professional to prepare family meals may be the go in busy periods. In the end it works out equivalent to takeaway and is a whole lot healthier

Social media management

Employing or contracting someone to help you manage your social media can really free up your time. Finding someone who is up to the task is the difficult part. There are several support groups on Facebook for social media managers. Keep your eye out and get to know people you feel might be a good fit for your business. There are some wonderful virtual assistant companies out there, but if your staff are based in a different country, you will need to supervise them carefully to ensure that the communication on your social media profiles is representative of your brand and culture. A skilled local virtual assistant may be a good investment to oversee your social media management.

Bookkeeping

Bookkeeping is one of those business chores many people love to hate. It's necessary, but can be painful for people who are big on ideas but short on patience for repetitive tasks. If bookkeeping is not your passion or your strength, this is an area where getting some help would be fairly easy to do. Freelance bookkeepers are always looking for new clients. Ask around your business networks to find someone who has a great reputation for number crunching.

Visual marketing

Visual marketing is important in the online space, particularly when it comes to product marketing. Visual social networks like Instagram are growing in popularity all the time, and if you're not tapping into these tools, you may struggle to get a foothold in a competitive marketplace. Fortunately there are fantastic tools and services you can draw upon. To outsource simple graphics projects, you can post a request on fiverr.com, or 99designs.com. If you want to DIY, there are timesaving websites like canva.com or picmonkey.com that can help you create awesome graphics to share on social media, use as marketing collateral and create presentations.

Website maintenance

The more technical aspects of running a business are one of the biggest areas of struggle for business owners. Looking after your website is one of these. Fortunately, there are virtual assistants who specialise in website support and you're sure to find someone who is right for your website if you look on elance.com or a similar contracting marketplace. If you have a Wordpress website, you may want to check out wpcurve.com, a business that provides dedicated Wordpress support on a month-by-month basis.

A note about outsourcing

With any company or service you aim to use, a quick Google background check is a good way to find out more about the business. Whenever anybody emails me out of the blue, I do a background check before responding. You really can't be too careful.

It's easy to feel like we know people online, but, unless we've met people in person, or at least have communicated with them on a regular basis, we really don't. So be careful and thorough when you're checking out a business and, conversely, don't be too quick to give recommendations. If you recommend someone without having experienced their customer service first hand and they end up letting the other person down, it could be damaging to your reputation.

Action Step

What aspect of your life or business can you get help with now? What do you need to do in order to make this happen? Make a checklist and stick it on the fridge!

3. Disorganised administration and management

Running a business means that you are responsible for every aspect of the business—bookkeeping, sales, accounting, HR, customer care, debt collection, technical support, marketing and administration. What if your business suddenly takes off and you need to outsource more or take on staff? What if you find you're doing the same documents over and over again? You can help yourself a lot by documenting how you do things as you go.

If you don't put systems in place and document how things are done, you will have a hard time teaching anyone else how to do what you do. This makes it difficult to outsource work to others. You have probably already developed unwritten procedures for repetitive tasks, so keep in mind that you may need to share these procedures with others.

Establishing set procedures will save a lot of time reinventing the wheel so you can put your time to better use. For instance, you could create a simple template for business proposals. Many clients want the same or similar services and have similar problems to address, so create a template for proposals that includes information common to most of your clients' needs. If something isn't relevant for a particular proposal, simply remove it.

There will always be aspects of your business that will run better if you map them out in great detail and create a process for them. An example might be how you put together a newsletter. Break it down step-by-step so that the process is easy for someone else to follow and implement. This can not only save you time and help you convey information to others you work with, but can also help you maintain a good reputation, particularly when procedures, or lack thereof, impact on customers' experience.

If you do everything on the fly you may not only feel a sense of panic about the tasks before you but you may end up conveying that sense of panic to others—employees, customers and potential joint-venture partners. Instead, create task lists, schedules and routines to help you get into good time-management habits.

If your work means talking to a variety of specialists such as programmers and marketing analysts who work with your clients or with you, then putting procedures in place to facilitate communication can mean a more productive environment for everyone.

One of the best books I have read that has helped me improve my administration and management was a book about leadership by mother of six and CEO, Alison Vidotto. Add *22 Leadership Fundamentals* to your must-read list for some down-to-earth inspiration. Gaining that bigger picture view of where I wanted my business to go and how I was going to make that happen was essential to the business's sustainability.

Action Steps

Take 15 minutes each day to organise your files, your emails and your systems. Once you're in the habit, you'll be amazed at how much better you feel.

As you do your work, take half an hour or so each day for a week to document how you did things. A great way to do this is to do a demo video using screen-recording software. That way you can easily catalogue tasks in a database for others to learn on demand.

4. You don't look for investment opportunities

There are many ways to fund a fledgling business and you may prefer to keep plugging along one step at a time so that you always own your business in its entirety. However, many startups struggle and then fall over when they could have benefited from external funding to get them through the initial stages. If your idea can be scaled (i.e. able to grow into something bigger and more profitable), investors will be interested, and even if it's not, there will be investors interested in your cause based on the values your business or service is about. So what kinds of investment opportunities are available for startups?

Bank loans

The most common funding source used by small businesses is the good ole bank. Small business loans are relatively easy to obtain. However, if your startup is information-based or based on human capital and not physical goods, it may be more difficult to attract funding and establish a track record with the bank.

Angel funding and venture capitalism

An angel investor or venture capitalist is a wealthy person or organisation that provides capital for startups. They may do this in exchange for equity in the business or shares later down the track. There are now several websites that help connect angel investors with entrepreneurs, for example, gust.com.

Crowdfunding

Crowdfunding is a relatively new kid on the block when it comes to financing business projects. The concept has only been around since the mid 2000s and involves asking for small amounts of money from large numbers of people to support a project. Websites such as kickstarter.com and indiegogo.com fund creative projects, and if you don't raise the required amount, your project doesn't get funded. Charities have now cottoned on to the crowdfunding idea and are using crowdfunding charity websites to further their causes. If you have a large following, or a grassroots project, crowdfunding may be a great way to go. If you are going to go down the crowdfunding road, make sure you can deliver what you promise within the time frame. The 2012 study *The Dynamics of Crowdfunding: Determinants of Success and Failure*, shows an astounding 75% of founders don't deliver their projects on time. The bottom line is, if you don't manage investor expectations well, you can seriously hamper your reputation.

Government grants

Governments in countries like the US, Australia and the UK are tuning in to the rising number of startups and there are several grants on offer through government agencies. Visit government websites to find out what is currently available in your country.

Joint ventures

As your business grows, you will find that more and more requests will come your way to collaborate on various projects. While it is great to be open to new relationships and projects, sometimes another person's agenda can get in the way of your business success, and, indeed, your life goals and priorities. Remember that integrity is important, not just for how you feel but for how your customers and clients feel. It is easy to get side-tracked by another person's agenda but if it doesn't fit with your purpose, business plan or philosophy, just say no.

Conversely, there may be businesses you are keen to align yourself with. Many small, internet-based businesses join affiliate programs for this reason. When looking at joint venture opportunities, it's best to first develop the relationships and second, see where the synergies are. If someone is very quick to want to partner with you, slow things down a little so you can get to know each other first.

⭐ Action Step

Subscribe to online magazines that feature funding opportunities and competitions and resolve to learn more about your options. Online magazines such as entrepreneur.com, inc.com, venturebeat.com and startupsmart.com.au regularly feature funding competitions and opportunities.

Un-Career Story

There are many ways to fund your fledgling business. A popular one is angel funding, however this involves giving part ownership of your business to another party. Nitty chose to work part time to supplement her business income as this allows her to keep complete control over the business. This choice is starting to pay off for Nitty.

Nitty's Story

When I first started my business I was on my second round of maternity leave. There wasn't a large gap between my first and second child and we didn't have the savings we'd had for our first one. The finances dried up quickly and as the business was in its first stages, what was coming in wasn't covering what was going out. The business income was going back into the business, and because I was an online business, I invested in my website. I realised that I need income to support the family, and found a part time position that complemented my business perfectly and fitted in to my lifestyle of kids, business and working. Looking back, the biggest challenge in business has been finding the funds to keep growing the business, as you need to spend money to make money.

I am quite a driven and passionate person and that has led me to work really hard to get my business up and running. I love what I do and I am good at it. My husband has been an amazing support through this business journey, he is the one who invested in my company as he knew how much I wanted to do it.

I love helping other small business owners. They work so hard to build their businesses and it is very competitive out there for my clients, who mainly sell at markets or online. Being able to promote them and give them advice on some great resources to help grow their business means a lot to me. I market my business by networking, building my brand through relationships, media, and taking part in opportunities that I come across.

I have finally managed to get a balance of family, personal, business and work life and am happier within myself. Working part time to supplement my business has taken a lot of pressure off. I have also hired a cleaner, which is one of the best decisions I have made as it reduces my stress.

As a business owner, you need a good support network behind you. Attend networking events and get to know other business people. It really is about building relationships. Save funds towards your business, as the reality is that it can take a few years before your business starts to make a profit. Good products and services cost money. If you are serious, you need to invest in quality. You may have bad days and think "What am I doing?" but think positive and tell yourself you can do it.

Nitty Brown from Markets and Community,
marketsandcommunity.com.au, lives in Melbourne, Victoria, Australia.

5. Not investing in mentoring or business coaching

Nobody knows everything and if you want to get ahead in business it pays to get up to speed on the things you don't know, and learn from others' experiences.

Investing in mentoring and coaching programs made the biggest difference to my marketing business's profitability. I gained clarity on my strengths and was able to systemise my knowledge to form courses so that the information I shared was easy for my clients to digest.

These days there is a plethora of online mentoring and coaching programs geared towards helping you grow your business. Investing in your business is a sign that you are ready to grow and take a leap of faith that the investment will pay off.

Here's what I've learned about working with business coaches and mentors:

Bigger does not necessarily mean better

Working with a prestigious or famous business coach does not necessarily translate into value for money for you. In the past two years I've worked with three different business coaches and by far the best one was the coach from a smaller business who offered small group training at an affordable rate and gave individual feedback on my progress.

There's often an upsell

A lot of business coaches do training programs where they learn how to leverage their lower-level programs to encourage people to step into higher-level programs. I know, because I've done one such course. It didn't sit right with me when I saw just how much the trainer was upselling during the $1000 program I did. It pays to be aware of this beforehand. Some business coaches do more upselling than others. Shop around and see who resonates with you before spending a lot of money on a business development program.

There's often a lot of hype

I cannot even begin to count the number of programs I've encountered that offer participants the keys to greater freedom, the lifestyle you want and loads of cash.

The Law of Attraction has become synonymous with achieving success. However, there are also six other laws... gravity being one of them. I would encourage you to stay grounded and not get carried away by the hype. Only 2% of women business owners are making millions, and this has hardly changed in the last ten years, even with women-owned businesses growing in number exponentially. It is wise to take a step back and retain some objectivity before diving into a new program selling the idea that if you dream it, it will happen. It's a great idea to set your intention and believe something will happen. However you must also be prepared to work hard and smart to achieve your goals. You make your life happen!

Action Step

Make a list of business coaches and mentors you would love to work with and then put them on interest lists on Facebook, a list on Twitter or circle them on Google Plus to keep tabs on their social media updates. This will help you ascertain whether or not different coaches and mentors are offering value for you.

Join a women's business organisation in your area, particularly one that runs a mentoring program.

6. Self-sabotaging beliefs about money and your earning potential

Running your own business does not mean you won't or can't make serious money! You can if you have the right mindset and the right structure in place.

It is easy to get caught up in the mindset that you can only go so far and earn so much because there are only so many hours in the day.

I often read the following on Facebook:

- "I'm not really making any money"
- "I'm just earning enough to..."
- "I know mums can't afford much"
- "I don't think anyone would pay more than that"
- "I'm a struggling work at home mum"

The problem is that with words like this, you limit yourself to thinking small, and restricting not only your audience's spending potential, but your own income potential.

Why does earning more have to mean working more or working in a corporate office? The truth is, it doesn't! If you're going to work so hard on your business, shouldn't you also be reaping the rewards and shouldn't you be expecting to?

Making peace with making money

When I was a little girl, my mother joined a religious sect similar to the Seventh Day Adventists. In the years that followed, our family's life was controlled by this organisation and it shaped my views on money to a huge degree. I used to think that money, or rather desiring money, was evil and selfish. I was told that 'our lot' shouldn't expect too much in terms of wealth or success. These things were not to be desired or sought after. Instead, I saw many families struggling to get by and yet still giving 10% of their income to a church whose leaders spent it on private jets and gold-lined cake at lavish parties.

For me, money, or lots of money, meant opulence, extravagance and profiteering. It represented oppression and power.

Although your own upbringing may not have been so extreme, the idea that it is somehow bad to have lots of money is fairly common.

In the years that followed my separation from this cult, I've made my peace with money. I've recognised that, in order to do more and create the change I want to see in the world, I need to have more freedom. But because money was not something I ever respected growing up, it's been a battle. I'm caught between the desire to keep things affordable for others and to keep life and work sustainable for my family.

After running my own business for a while, in 2012 I had an epiphany. I realised that many women undervalue their worth and their potential, but by doing so, they also enable others to devalue their worth too. It's why housewives have long been patronised for their contributions to communities, and now I'm finding the same is true with mum entrepreneurs. The term "mumpreneur" is controversial because on the one hand some women find it patronising and on the other some women find it empowering. I think the use of this term is a sign of our changing entrepreneurial culture. Mums used to feel that their only choices were stay home or go to work. Now, because entrepreneurship has become more accessible, women feel their choices have expanded. This can only be a good thing.

An unhealthy attitude toward wealth creation is particularly noticeable in the health and wellbeing arena. A Facebook group conversation between fellow birth doulas became really heated because someone was talking about raising their fees. There was a judgment hanging in the air that if you put your prices up, you are more about serving your own interests than the interests of the women you help. Many doulas don't charge more than $1500 for a birth, even though, if you broke that down, it would work out to about $5 an hour for some births. I've noted that many in the wellbeing industry have to have sideline jobs so they can sustain their practices. This just shouldn't be the case. Whatever your line of work, you can truly serve your ideal clients without burning out and without putting a strain on your family.

> The bottom line is, people buy based on perceived value, not on price.

The thing is, when you price your services according to what you think people are willing to pay or can afford, you may be creating the perception that your services aren't valuable. And yet, there isn't one birth client I knew of who thought that after their baby's birth. I commonly heard the phrase "You should charge more for what you do because it's priceless." The bottom line is, people buy based on perceived value, not on price.

Pricing considerations

When you are working out pricing for your products and services, take into consideration the following:

- Cost of supplies

- How much you want to earn annually

- How many hours a week you want to work

- Cost of marketing products and services (advertising, website, printed materials etc.)

- Cost of business expenses and utilities (internet use, insurance, electricity etc.)

- A wholesale price and a retail price. The two price points give you room to offer sales and promotions off your retail price

- Number of years' experience you have

- Quality of your work

- Your level of expertise

Establish how much profit you want to make on each item or service and price accordingly. Many creative designers do not charge for their time. However, if you create art or products for a living, I'd encourage you to value your time. People buy unique handmade and designer-made products because they have emotional value. Also, studies show a trend towards buying eco-friendly, fair trade and handmade goods over mass-produced manufactured items made by big, faceless corporations.

Make sure your branding fits with your price points. If you have branding that looks unprofessional but you're asking high prices, it sends the wrong message. If you have beautiful branding but the quality of your work is not of a high calibre, this will also create a disparity for your potential clients.

Action Step

After reflecting on the pricing considerations above, ask yourself if you are charging enough. What can you do to showcase your value to potential buyers so they are not buying based on price?

7. Focusing on the competition

Focusing on what your competitors are doing distracts you from serving your ideal clients. Keep in mind that your competitors have different ideal clients to you. They serve a different crowd, even if there are similarities. If you are truly focused on serving your own ideal clients, you will attract them, and they won't go to your competitors. Those that do were never yours to begin with, so let them go with your blessing.

Copycatting

There is no doubt that copycatting is rife on the internet. My business models for two businesses have been copied. I've even seen people use the same words that are on my website. When I used to sell on Etsy, it was only a matter of time before someone took one of my precious ideas and started undercutting me.

These days, I don't worry about copycatting as much as I used to. Why? Because nobody can truly copy me. They don't have the same back story, the same essence or the same ideas. I trust that consumers are more savvy these days. They know when someone is really into their creations or services. They know when someone is truly passionate about what they do and they soon find out if someone is telling lies.

Breach of copyright

Another thing that is rife on the internet is breach of copyright. You may well find your articles and visuals on other people's blogs. It might seem like a compliment, but if you've put your heart and soul into your words and original content, it's annoying when people are disrespectful of your copyright.

If you are concerned about breaches of copyright of your blog posts or your website, there are a couple of simple things you can do:

- Do regular checks on copyscape.com for your copy. Copyscape.com compares copy on the internet. If it finds a match, you can look up the offending website and send them a cease and desist notice

- Put trackbacks in blog posts and do internal linking. Every blog post you write should have links back to other content on your website. People who copy your blog don't always check for links back to your website so you'd still be getting some benefit from it. If you have trackbacks turned on in Wordpress, you will be notified when someone re-blogs your copy. In some cases this may be legitimate, for instance if they've linked to your blog and written a commentary about how wonderful it was. That's worth tracking in itself! When it isn't legitimate, you'll be able to check it out thoroughly and contact the offending party about either giving due credit or taking down the blog post

Action Step

If you have a blog already, go through your website and add internal links in your blog posts.

Write an affirmation about your uniqueness and stick it on your bathroom mirror. Remind yourself each day that you and your essence cannot be copied.

8. No systems in place to protect your brand and frame your growth

Whether you are a solo business owner or the leader of a small team, you need systems and mechanisms in place to act as a guardrail for when things don't go smoothly. Having a privacy policy and website terms of use covers you legally should someone hack your website or mailing list.

To protect your brand, establishing a trademark is a must. Start by establishing a track record of brand usage and then apply for your trademark through whatever governing body issues them in your country. You can also apply for international trademarks. For more information about trademarks, contact an intellectual property lawyer who works specifically in this area.

Having accounting and debt collection policies in place helps you manage your customers' expectations and also recover unpaid invoices. At some point, someone will fail to pay you for your work and you need to have a plan for pursuing it, or you'll be missing out on income you have rightfully earned. If you aren't personally comfortable with playing both sales person and debt collector, two very opposite roles, you may want to hire someone to undertake debt collection on your behalf. Ask your business networks for referrals to qualified debt collectors. In some circumstances, you may feel you're better off to let the debt go and simply choose not to do any further business with that person. Whatever path you decide to take, commit to it and either pursue or let it go.

Action Step

Ask your networks for a referral to a trademark specialist so you can take action and get your brand trademarked.

Write a list of what areas of your business need a policy, and make a plan to create this. Some common policy areas are: social media management, website terms of use, privacy and customer service.

9. Rushing into investing in services that don't deliver what they promise

In my time as a business owner and mentor I've seen fledgling businesses make costly mistakes. It's easy to do when you don't know the lay of the virtual land. While businesses can over (and under) invest in lots of things, here are the five most common areas where businesses either invest too much or too little.

1. SEO development

If someone insists that the key to your online marketing success lays with spending thousands on SEO, run away as fast as you can. SEO is not as complex as the SEO scammers would have you believe. If you want to rank number one on Google for your chosen keywords, you may need to invest a little to get some help identifying what keywords will work for your business, but you definitely don't need to invest thousands. When I was trying to get my head around how SEO worked I used Scribe SEO software from studiopress.com and it worked just fine. Yes, maybe my websites could be ranking better on some keywords, but I don't focus on this as a solution to my online marketing.

Word of mouth is still king when it comes to business referrals, and social media amplifies word of mouth exponentially. If you are doing social media marketing well, you don't need to be so concerned about organic search. If you are looking for an SEO expert to help you with your keywords, make sure they are ethical and follow best practice. There are many SEO specialists that try to game Google and in the end that means you will have wasted your money. Google tweaks its search algorithms all the time and the main thing I've noticed is that the newer algorithms favour genuinely authoritative, helpful content. Being on Google+ will also boost your search engine rankings. Google wants to know you're a real person sharing real information, and the more regularly you share in the form of blog posts and original content, the better that will be for your search engine rankings.

2. Websites

Having your own website is the only way to ensure you have ultimate control over your content. You rent space on Facebook and other platforms, you don't own it. Establishing a free website might get you kick-started but it's not a good permanent solution, especially if free means having ads on your website that might not be a good fit for your business. Conversely, spending thousands on a website is not necessarily the answer either. Some unscrupulous web designers can leave a small business up the river without a proverbial paddle by failing to provide appropriate training and support or by creating pretty websites that don't convert into leads and sales. It's a good idea to shop around and find someone who has good recommendations from people you know and trust. I recommend building a small business website on the Wordpress self-hosted platform because it is easy to DIY, designers who develop on Wordpress don't charge an arm and a leg and it enables you to hook into a plethora of useful business plugins.

3. Online marketing

There are many reputable online marketing services out there but there are some that are, quite frankly, dodgy. Beware of the hype and look at the results people get. It helps to know people who have experienced good results with a digital marketing agency or consultant. Look at the consultant's track record and check out their social profiles. How are they performing?

4. Wealth creation

I've lost count of the number of wealth creation schemes there are online. It seems that just about everyone has the keys to wealth, success and happiness. The truth is they don't, and sometimes perfectly sensible people can be led to buy into things like Ponzi schemes and the like. There are no secret, miraculous ways to create wealth. It takes timeliness, tenacity and a lot of know-how. That last bit, know-how, often means a lot of research and a lot of education. It means making the right connections with the right people and offering something of value. Don't buy into hype! You will regret it. You have been warned.

5. Industry membership programs

Industry membership programs can be terrific, if they are active and involve lots of interaction and crucial knowledge-sharing, but they can also be a bit light on value. If you're going to join a membership program, make sure that it will add value to your business, bring you new referrals and help you create rapport with new potential clients and peers. If all you get is a quarterly magazine and the opportunity to sign up for expensive business breakfasts, perhaps there is another way to get your networking needs met.

How to identify services that will provide you value

If you're looking for services that will add value to your business, there are a few rules of thumb that will help you sort valuable opportunities from time and money-wasting ploys.

Follow them for a few months before engaging

Is the business or person active on social media? How are they communicating and when are they communicating? For example, if the only time you hear from a rock-star social media trainer is when they have a program to launch, but they claim to have crucial insider knowledge on social media, take that as a sign that you should look elsewhere for mentorship on this topic.

What do others say about them?

Before committing to services or adopting a new software platform in your business, ask around your networks to see what others' experiences have been. Check out the business's social media pages to see what feedback customers and clients are leaving. Take your time and don't rush into decisions, even if the business makes time-sensitive offers. There will always be another time to take them up on an offer.

How much hype is in their emails and sales pages?

When I see a sales page or email that's full of hype, urgent call-to-action statements and salesy graphics, I run the other way. Some businesses are really good at making you feel like you must take action now. Sometimes this is a good thing and sometimes, it can leave you wondering why on earth you pulled your credit card out when you did. Leave the credit card in your purse and scrutinise sales pages to see what's in it for you. If the benefits are vague, that's a sign you should perhaps move on to something else.

How do they compare to their competitors?

When looking for business services, you want to compare apples with apples. Have a look at how the business compares with other similar services. Check out the testimonials and see if they have a blog with case studies. If you can't find the answers right away, contact them and ask questions. You'd be amazed at how many people don't do this one simple thing.

Ask your networks for referrals to SEO programs or professionals who can help you sort out your keywords.

Look up three Wordpress developers on Facebook or Twitter and follow them to start checking them out.

Make a list of business membership programs you're interested in and compare the benefits. Are they offering you value? Will they result in increased referrals or professional development opportunities? If not, cross them off the list.

When you're considering a new service, check for referrals from people you know and trust and track their social media activity. Are they full of hype or are they for real?

Un-Career Story

If you can't find a business organisation or community to join, you can always start one. That's what tea-preneur May King Tsang did.

May King's Story

My parents did their utmost to ensure we had a good education and encouraged us to work hard towards establishing a career. It was the work ethic instilled in me from a young age that enabled me to work my way up my IT career before an opportunity presented itself for me to start my own business.

A friend asked if I'd like to start a coffee shop bringing together art, music and coffee. My first business lesson came when I went to a large coffee chain for research on our business, I realised I had no idea about coffee, but I had been drinking tea ever since my parents took the family out to have Yum Cha (or Dim Sum as we know it in the UK) and was also a fan of milk and two sugars tea. That was when I had my 'eureka' moment: it was tea I wanted to go into, not coffee. My friend and I had a different vision for the tea business during the focus group testing phase, and so we went our separate ways, but we are still very good friends.

I continued my research through books and training courses, and gained my qualification with the Specialty Tea Institute as Australia and the UK's only certified Tea Specialist. I realised I had found my calling, encouraged by reading books that told me if you have a passion for something then this would be a great start for your business. In one month I read eight of these books! Passion for tea was the impetus for me to make the leap from the corporate world to owning my own business, pushed along by being made redundant a few months after launching MayKing Tea in London.

My corporate world experience and work ethic helped me along my business journey, but the book that had the biggest impact on me was Dale Carnegie's *How To Win Friends and Influence People*. I realised I had been doing this all my life, and the book helped me see how I could use this skill to make a difference to my business. This made me smile; I felt like the book gave me permission to be myself, so when I met with other business owners I wouldn't have to go for the hard sell and thrusting of business cards into people's hands, which is what I envisaged being in business would be about.

The biggest challenge for me as a solo business owner is doing those things in my business that I don't enjoy. In the corporate world, I was hired to manage a team. Being a small business owner, at the beginning, one has to be the marketing person, sales and forecasting, the admin person, the trainer, the finance person, customer service, the HR person, and, of course, the owner. When you are in a position to be able to outsource some of those tasks, that frees up a lot of one's time, but at the start, it can be challenging not to get overwhelmed and end up procrastinating. I was encouraged to read *Eat That Frog*, a book about how to stop procrastinating by Brian Tracy. The title still makes me giggle and when I feel myself in a space of overwhelm, I remember the title to help me push through.

When I go into a café or restaurant and find the traditional square teabags are still on the beverages menu, this inspires me to continue with my work.

Ten years ago, I believe coffee in Australia found itself in a similar situation with its instant counterpart, and look at where we are now with so many coffees available to the consumer. I believe that with the age of social media, and with Starbucks, Unilever, Coca-Cola and even Oprah Winfrey getting into the tea game, tea is most certainly the new coffee.

When I moved to Brisbane in 2010, I didn't know a single person, so I devised a relationship-building strategy via networking events and social media. Twitter was my main platform, and I was consequently invited to write for three different tea blogs as well as my own. It helped the blogs as they received quality content, and it helped to raise my global profile. Collaborations are what I am good at; I find that working with like-minded business owners provides a win-win for both parties. Being in business for oneself can often be a lonely place, so having an opportunity to work with others is, let's face it, a lot more fun! Make sure you find the right partners to work with though. I have often been in partnerships where it was the expectation that I would do all the work and share half of the profits!

Relationship building takes time but the efforts are rewarding. I owe my success in this area to using social media effectively. Remember, I started without knowing a single sausage when I moved to Brisbane.

I had many naysayers tell me that I couldn't make money out of relationship building and social media but now the networking group I started in 2010, the Queensland Business Group, has nearly 5000 members. I'd like to raise my thumb to my nose, wave my four fingers Mexican-wave style and sing "nernernernerner," respectfully of course.

When working in the corporate space, I didn't achieve a work-life balance, preferring to work 90+ hours, and I've struggled to achieve work-life balance as a solo business owner too, but I enjoy what I do, so sometimes it's hard to cut back. There's also a lot more pressure to perform when you work for yourself. In the corporate world, there was a guaranteed wage at the end of the month. When you are starting out in business, you may experience a good month followed by a not-so-good month and this can often put pressure on the family, so communicating with loved ones is extremely important.

If you're considering leaving the corporate world to start your own business, do your research, learn from other business owners and do not listen to the naysayers. Naysayers sometimes love you dearly and don't want you to fail, but if you are equipped with the right knowledge and passion and hang out with like-minded business owners, you will be on the biggest rollercoaster of your life. There will be downs but focus on the ups and, as my UK business mentor once told me, celebrate all successes, no matter how small.

May King Tsang is the founder of May King Tea,
founder of Queensland Business Group, queenslandbusinessgroup.com,
and co-founder of The Likeability Company, thelikeabilityco.com.
She currently lives in Brisbane, Queensland, Australia.

10. Not believing in yourself

When my eldest son was a new teen, we went camping at an incredible farm stay that had a three-metre-high diving board over a lake. The kids loved it!

It's a funny thing, the game your mind plays with you when you're standing on the edge of a three metre-high diving board. What was effortless for my kids seemed insurmountable to me. I watched as children raced each other up the ladder and then ran and jumped into the water below with a "Yeehah!"

Eventually, I had courage enough to climb the ladder, but as I stood up the top, the dizziness set in. It was high. Very high! I hadn't jumped off anything higher than one metre since I was 20. What the heck was I doing?

Then the thought occurred to me. I don't need to do this just because everyone else is. So, I climbed down and forgot about it for a while.

Meanwhile, my eight-year-old climbed up the ladder and stood there for what seemed like an eternity.

I watched as he went through the process. First, other kids tried to encourage him. Then, they tried to cajole him. He just stood there, attached to the nearest pole.

You can stop yourself from doing anything just by thinking about it.

Then, all of a sudden, after a number of false starts, he declared, "Geronimo!" and ran and jumped into the water, three metres below.

Everyone cheered!

My eight-year-old had done what I couldn't bring myself to do, but what struck me was that he simply made a decision to do it.

So, I knew that before the day was done, I had to do it too - not to please anyone else, just to prove to myself I could. I waited until I thought no one was watching, climbed the ladder and walked to the edge of the diving board.

The kids were laughing and playing with a tyre tube on the other side of the lake, but all of a sudden, it went quiet. One of the girls looked up and pointed, afraid that if she said anything, I wouldn't jump. And then it happened. I just stepped off, screamed, made a clumsy attempt to block my nose, and hit the water. When I surfaced, everyone was cheering. I did it!

The mind is a funny thing. You can stop yourself from doing anything just by thinking about it. You'll go through the motions of trying to work out what's the worst that can happen, but true courage is when you know all this and do it anyway.

I jumped off that diving board another three times, and the last time I overbalanced and smacked my face. Ouch! Yes it hurt, but I put that one down to experience. Sometimes when you jump, you'll smack your face and come away with a bruise, but you'll live and you'll learn from the experience, so you can jump another day.

My thought was, well, if I die jumping off this diving board... what a way to go!

> Each leap of faith has resulted in change and growth. I am stronger, wiser and more able to take the leap again. Don't let fear hold you back!

Problogger's Darren Rowse once said "Fear comes before great change." I have definitely found this to be true for me. Over the past few years I've faced a lot of fear, and great changes have followed. In my time as a business owner I've pushed myself to do things that were way out of my comfort zone, like talking to people at networking events, creating Youtube videos, learning a new technical skill or even making some difficult and heartbreaking personal decisions. In every case, I was fearful of taking the leap, of what would happen afterwards. The incredible thing is that each leap of faith has resulted in change and growth. I am stronger, wiser and more able to take the leap again. Don't let fear hold you back!

Un-Career Story

Fear can drive inaction but it can also lead us into the unknown and unpredictable world of action. Amanda Hoffmann shares her story about how she overcame her fears to startup a successful student accommodation business.

Amanda's Story

I hated my job - the hours, the monotony, catching public transport, abiding by the hours given to me by upper management. I was doing shift work that no one else wanted and I had to accept it because I had no children and could be more flexible.

I felt physically sick as I entered the office door each day, except for the day I took a deep breath, walked into upper management's office and resigned.

Oh, the liberation, the feeling of freedom as I practically skipped out of that building knowing I never, ever had to return!

What I did not know was, since I was no longer working, hubby had other plans for me. My husband's friend and former housemate had just gone through a difficult divorce. Financially and emotionally this man was crushed, so what did my husband do? He spent $40,000 setting up a pest control and carpet cleaning business with van, machines and advertising, to help his friend make a new start.

However, an insidious dark, disturbing feeling of depression was choking the life out of my husband's friend and suffocating his chance for success. Jobs were not completed and customers were angry. I skipped out of the frying pan of one job, straight into the fire of answering phone calls, booking jobs and managing complaints.

It was here that I learned two very important lessons:

1. Money loaned to a friend or family member should not come with an expectation of repayment.
2. Friendship and business, when mixed, will eventually lead to loss of both.

This difficult period wasn't without reward - I discovered an entrepreneurial spirit as I stepped forward to become Queensland's first female carpet cleaner and pest controller.

The business boomed. Women loved a female coming to their homes to clean their carpets and do their pest control. I worked two or three days a week and made three times what I had full-time.

All was going well until I had my first, then my second miscarriage. I was worried that although I had been incredibly careful with regular blood screening, and looked like a spacewoman when spraying pesticide, my work had contributed to my miscarriages. Upon my third pregnancy, I sold the business.

Motherhood is incredibly rewarding. I love my children and spending time with them. For me however, this was not enough to make me happy. I needed more than nappies, dishes, laundry, domestic work and cooking. My self-esteem was taking a dive and the universe had taken note.

So, what did I do about it? I read Robert Kiyosaki's *Rich Dad, Poor Dad*, as well as books by Dale Carnegie, Anthony Robbins and Stephen R Covey. I found out about an overseas convention where sophisticated investors and experienced professionals were holding workshops on wealth creation.

It was here that I started to see business not just as a job, but a tool to achieve financial independence.

When, one day, I overheard university students complaining about the condition of their share house and how difficult it was to find accommodation that was comfortable and clean, I saw an opportunity.

I researched, learned all I could from other property investors, played the game *Cash Flow* and then proceeded to put what I had learned into practice.

I recall sitting in my bank manager's waiting room. I was nervous to the point I had been sick several times leading up to my appointment. My hands were sweating and shaking. I had spent months completing my due diligence, sourcing an appropriate house in the right area that was walking distance to university, shops and transport. I had calculated out a forecast of expenses, income, management, how I would fill all the rooms and keep the property occupied to meet mortgage repayments.

My husband had told me that he was willing to stay home to look after the three small boys, but that it was my idea and I had to present my investment business plan to the bank on my own merit.

The bank manager was polite and somewhat disinterested. We sat down as I began to explain the purpose of my visit. His disinterest changed before my eyes. I saw respect as he read my business plan, then genuine interest quickly turned into enthusiasm.

He smiled and reached out to shake my hand as he told me, "Congratulations, your pre-approval is granted".

As I shook his hand, a strong emotion of fear washed over me. I looked him in the eyes and said "No!"

Confused, he sat down and asked, "What do you mean by no?"

I started to cry, I expressed my feelings truthfully that I was overwhelmed by the amount of money that had just been approved.

Calmly, the bank manager reaffirmed, "Your loan will be approved, your strategy is well thought out, to a point that I personally wish I had thought of it."

It was over ten years ago that Kidd House Accommodation, a student accommodation and share housing rental business, was born. It has grown to a multi-million dollar business today. Turnkey systems continue to develop, and personality profiling and cultural compatibility assists with tenant retention. In some cases it has been so successful that tenants have even gotten married.

Systems, genuine interest, patience and professionalism all contribute to Kidd House Accommodation's quiet success. It is a family-run operation and not highly publicised.

It is our financial source of future independence. It has sustained growth in spite of a fluctuating Australian dollar, immigration and visa changes, local council law upgrades and compliance requirements.

If you have a dream, then research, gather your information, plan and present it. Move forward with action in spite of your own fears. You can and will grow with your success and in the end, the only thing that will hold you back, is yourself!

Amanda Hoffman from Kidd House Accommodation,
kiddhouseaccommodation.com.au, lives in Brisbane,
Queensland, Ausralia.

Bonus: Download bonus resources that dig deeper into this topic. For this chapter, I interviewed Alison Vidotto, CEO of the Vidotto Group, founder of Australian charity Children of Vietnam and founder of PUSH Leadership, on how to avoid common business pitfalls. There's also a free Business Barriers worksheet to help you navigate the potholes on your business journey and a printable affirmation to inspire you to take action now. To access these bonus resources, simply sign up here: bit.ly/uncareerresources

Chapter 4

Creating your path to happiness, freedom and success

When I was 18 and about to embark on an adventure overseas, my grandmother gave me a small book to document my travels. However, I had other plans for that little book; it became a goal book. I neatly segmented it into categories and wrote down every goal I could think of. They included:

- Stand on the top of the Eiffel Tower in Paris

- Get a decent SLR camera

- Travel through at least 25 states in America

- Record my own original CD

and more...

And you know what, I crossed off most of the goals in that book, including all of the above by the time I was 32.

I've always been goal-oriented and a bit ambitious, but lately I've been examining my motivations and rethinking what it is I want to achieve in the years ahead. Again, it all comes down to that overarching *why*.

When I started up my first small business, I really just wanted to do something I loved and earn some extra income to help pay for the kids' activities and the occasional holiday. But it was through the process of starting up that I discovered my business legs, and as I gained confidence and soaked up knowledge, I realised that the sky was truly the limit.

As other women around me were starting to create wealth and experience great success, I enthusiastically jumped on the money-making bandwagon. My focus shifted from doing what I loved for the reasons I loved doing it, to chasing the promise of future happiness, wealth and freedom. I lost track of my *why* and started chasing rainbows.

Not long ago, I attended the birth of a baby boy as a birth doula. The joy on my client's face and the ease with which she found her feet with her new baby made me happy, and all the money in the world could not replace that feeling.

Recently in another of my businesses, a marketing client wrote to me to let me know that she was making more money and enjoying greater success as a result of working with me. I was overjoyed!

In an age where so many gurus sell the myth that 'making money means being happy', where we are tempted by ideas that promise we will catch that rainbow, it's easy to get side-tracked from what is truly important to you and what makes your business unique, authentic and fun now.

The thing is, if you aren't happy doing what you're doing now, and being who you are now, that rainbow will keep teasing you from afar.

You have enormous potential, and I definitely believe you should uncover that potential, but it's worth taking a good, hard look at why you're doing what you're doing, because if you're not doing it for reasons that are meaningful to you, your chances of reaching that pot of gold are slim.

With this in mind, let's talk about what you can do to both love the life you're living in the now and, at the same time, create your path to happiness, freedom and success in business.

Are you creating a business or a hobby?

Before you can create your path to happiness, freedom and success, it's a good idea to pinpoint the things that might be holding you back from achieving your best success. One question that needs answering is: what am I trying to build—a business or a hobby?

Make a decision and move in the direction that best suits your needs. If you want to add value to your family life by doing something you love, and making a profit isn't a high priority, that's a hobby. A hobby is about sustaining your interests. If you're not making a profit, it's a hobby. However if you are working hard so you can make a living, then you need your business to be profitable.

To have a truly brilliant un-career, jumping across the ravines yelling "Geronimo!" is the way to move forward.

There is absolutely nothing wrong with having a hobby business. However, if you want to make a profit, you cannot approach your business as if it were a hobby. Stepping into the next stage of your business growth can be challenging and scary, but once you do it, you'll never look back. To have a truly brilliant un-career, jumping across the ravines yelling "Geronimo!" is the way to move forward.

Un-Career Story

Like many entrepreneurs, PR and Marketing Coach Linda Reed-Enever had a lot of irons in the fire, juggling a busy work life with caring for a young family. Linda's suggestion for those looking to take an un-career move is not to make excuses but to dive in and 'do it'.

Linda's Story

After a two and half year IVF journey, I was motivated to leave the corporate world with the birth of my daughter.

For me it was time for me to call the shots on who and what I worked with and on.

My IVF journey made this easy for me as I started consulting just after we got married, allowing me to work project to project and to take away the worry of 'what if I fall pregnant on the corporate ladder?' If I am honest, I had already climbed this ladder, and it was time to stop.

My amazing husband Clive is my mentor, best friend and greatest support. Without him, I would not have created the business community I have, and I am lucky enough really to love what I do!

My first non-corporate job was founding small business e-zine *Family Capers* with Clive in 2009. Gone were the 'you can't do thats' and the doors opened along with opportunities.

This was my project, and I had full control over its goals and outcomes. As *Family Capers* grew, my love of PR was nagging at me, and in late 2011 I founded my own agency, ThoughtSpot PR. I also started work on building Media Connections, a service that connects business owners with journalists.

So now with three businesses, the challenge for me became time. Finding time to roll out the ideas and vision I have for my businesses while working with amazing clients is hard.

In 2013, I stepped out of the editor's seat at *Family Capers* to focus on Media Connections to give me that time I needed.

I love what I do, but often that means my time gets eaten into, and I need to get better at saying no. As a business owner, we need to know that it is OK to say no and walk away. Not all business will be good for us.

New ideas and meeting new people keeps me inspired. Just when I think I have seen everything in the market, along comes a new idea or product to keep me going! I just love connecting. Often it will be a news release or client that picks me up when I am down. I get caught up in their dream and off I go again!

Naturally, I market my business mostly through PR and networking. I have built my profile through workshops and contributions to industry magazines and blogs, as well as traditional PR and marketing methods.

I still find face to face and a good old phone call the best way to get results, BUT you also need to have the online profile to back you up.

It took me a while to realise that you need to create office hours and educate your clients about these. Just because you work from home does not make you available 24/7. Value your time and charge appropriately for it. If you keep giving things away, people will keep taking.

Remember that your family needs you and that you need focused time with them outside office hours, just as you would if you were working. The best thing I did was move my office into a room where I could shut the door, that way I could walk away from the phone and email, and enjoy moments with my family.

If you're thinking about starting your own business, have your plans in place. It will make the tough days easier. You will have bad days just as you do now in a job. Don't let them get you down. Keep going and make decisions. Network and find yourself a great support group. Just DO IT! You will never know if you don't give it a try, and life is too short for 'what if I had' moments.

Linda Reed-Enever from Media Connections and ThoughtSpot PR
lindareedenever.com.au lives in Bendigo, Victoria, Australia

Developing an action plan, not just a business plan

When you come up with an idea for a business, you might think that the first thing you need to do is start writing a business plan. In the past I may have agreed with you, but not so now. The study *Pre-Startup Formal Business Plans and Post-Startup Performance: A Study of 116 New Ventures* published in the Venture Capital Journal assessed the performance of 116 new ventures. The study showed that startups that wrote comprehensive business plans did not perform better than those that didn't write a business plan.

I believe in business planning but not in the traditional sense.

Thousands of startup entrepreneurs start with a lot of zeal but little nuts and bolts structure to what they do. Sometimes it's the opposite, they have too much structure and too little passion. If you don't have the mix just right, your chances of going belly up are pretty high.

Too much passion and too little structure equals gaping holes and impending disaster.

Too much structure and too little passion equals inaction.

How do you get the mix right?

Firstly, forget fancy projection graphs and the like, and start with a set of actionable goals. You don't have a magic wand, so without an action plan, your pretty graphs will not translate into outcomes.

Here are a couple of questions to help you get started:

If you were being introduced at an event, what would the introduction say?

> "Here's Julie Adams from Adams Apple Chocolate Company. Julie is known for creating healthy chocolate even dentists love. Her delicious chocolate is known and loved throughout the world."

What do you see yourself doing in five years' time?

Are you sitting behind a desk with piles of paperwork before you or are you out celebrating your five years in business with your high-end clients and co-workers?

Now that you've imagined how you see yourself in five years' time, start thinking about some of the goals that you need to have in place in order to make that picture a reality. Give those goals a use-by date so you have a better chance of reaching them in good time. A great book for further reading on the topic of goal setting is Jack Canfield's *The Success Principles*.

Hypothetical case study

Meet Lynda, a clinical psychologist who is setting up a consulting room from her home office. Lynda wants to develop an action plan for her business. She starts by setting a goal and giving it a use-by date.

'By March 8, 2017, Lynda will be checking into the Waldorf Astoria Hotel in New York City to deliver her keynote address on women and depression to the International Psychological Association.'

Now Lynda has an achievable goal. Next, she needs to make it happen

How to make your goals actionable

An actionable business plan will break down goals into the following components:

Objectives

An objective is more specific than a goal. It is your goal broken down into measurable steps that each take you closer to achieving your goal. Objectives differ to goals in that they are specific, actionable targets for you to cross off your list. They help you achieve your overall goals.

For Lynda's goal, an objective could be:

- Launch a breakthrough program to help women beat depression, by March 8, 2015

Next, establish actions that need to be taken to make the objective happen.

Strategy

A strategy is the how you will achieve each objective. Strategy statements are action statements.

Lynda's strategies were:

- Write a signature program aimed at depressed women between the age of 30 and 45, by January 1, 2015

- Create a launch campaign involving collaborative launch partners, by February 12, 2015

Tactics

Tactics are strategies broken down into smaller components.

For Lynda's strategy to 'create a launch campaign involving collaborative launch partners by February 12, 2015', some of her tactics might be:

- Create a landing page and other marketing collateral by January 15, 2015

- Write launch partner emails and prepare resources for launch partners by January 30, 2015

- Create an email campaign in Infusionsoft by February 1, 2015

- Set date and venue for live launch event by February 12, 2015

In the following diagram I show the flow of action plan creation. Measurement, evaluation and research occur throughout the action-taking process. Smaller tactics help you achieve your broader strategies and objectives, and eventually your goal.

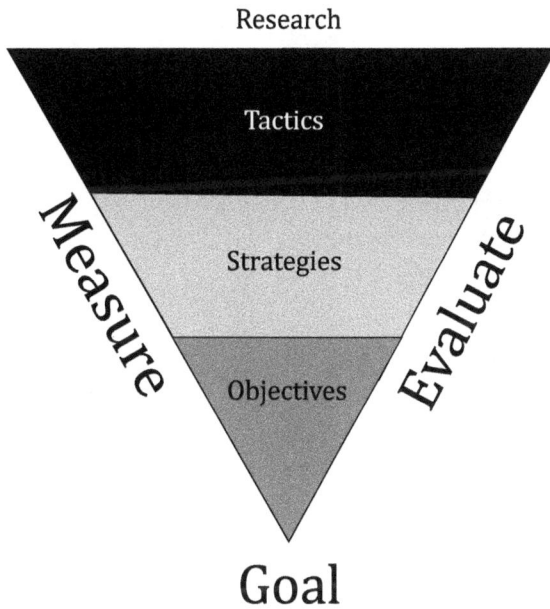

Research

Tactics

Strategies

Measure

Evaluate

Objectives

Goal

Evaluation

Ensuring each of your goals, objectives and strategies has a use-by date or a monetary figure attached to it will make each measurable. Give yourself a timeline and evaluate your progress as you go. Keep a journal to chart your progress and make notes on what you've learned along the way.

Avoiding tactical reactions

It's common to start implementing tactics without first setting a goal. This means there is no clear vision for where you want to be and what you want to be known for.

The problem with this approach is that you end up marketing your business in a highly reactive way, rather than setting the agenda for what you want to achieve and working towards it.

Establishing a goal and working your way from there down to more specific tasks and tactics will ensure your business plan is not only purpose-driven, but actionable steps as well.

Even the smallest of businesses can design a business plan in this way.

Un-Career Story

Jane shares how she put in the leg work and research to start her food business. Five years down the track, Jane is enjoying the fruits of her labour in a sustainable business she loves.

Jane's Story

After 20 years in the corporate arena, I was running the office of a Collins Street consulting firm in Melbourne when I realised the corporate road I'd mapped out was not going to plan. I'd always had an interest in food, but didn't have the opportunity to follow that passion when I was younger. I felt like it was the perfect time to explore that avenue. I quit my job, earned a Commercial Cookery Certificate then worked in hospitality for the next ten years.

Living overseas for a short time gave me the opportunity to explore options for my return. When researching kitchens for hire, I came across a business in the US that I wanted to model, a kitchen incubator. My Other Kitchen was built to provide a safe place for anyone starting out in the food industry. Those with a passion for what they make can get the help they need to turn it into a business idea. We provide business help in-house, and referrals to other experts such as web design, graphic design, packaging, food technology and marketing.

The success of my clients keeps me motivated. Being able to help them get over the hurdles of starting a new business is extremely rewarding. Although everyone walks the same journey, they all find different stages challenging. Keeping my business at the front of mind while contributing to other peoples' success is my biggest challenge. In particular, I struggle to work on the day-to-day tasks of business management.

Being a services business, my clients are my biggest fans, and word of mouth is invaluable. Keeping connected on social media and being grateful for the business that comes my way, seems to generate some interest. The best electronic marketing I do is with my website. Most of my clients have found me through searching online for small business help or commercial kitchen hire.

My husband is my number one supporter and the one I go to for help when I'm drowning in the business. This was never the case when we worked in the same industry. Working in separate industries has brought us closer together, and we allow for times when his job has to be the focus or my business intrudes on personal time. In the end, it's all good as long as we are aware of it.

I can tell you that I've never worked as hard, for so little pay (in the setup) or for so much reward as I do in my own business - and I LOVE IT!

Jane Del Rosso from My Other Kitchen myotherkitchen.com.au lives in Melbourne, Victoria, Australia.

Action Step

What goals do you have for your business? Take ten minutes right now to sit down and go through the goal setting process above. See how it can help you turn your dreams into action.

Bonus: Download bonus resources that dig deeper into this topic. For this chapter, I interviewed Dan Norris, author of The 7 Day Startup and Co-Founder of WPcurve.com. There's also a free Create Your Path template to help you get started on your un-plan and a printable affirmation to inspire you to take action now. To access these bonus resources, simply sign up here: bit.ly/uncareerresources

Chapter 5

Where to base your business

One of the big decisions facing you when you leave behind the corporate world is where to base your business. More often than not, new enterprises start out on the kitchen bench or the home office and then grow. With the growth in solo business ventures has come workplace and workspace innovation. Co-ops and other shared workspaces have sprung up everywhere for those who need a space outside the home to get their work done. Along with this have come some challenges, particularly where the lack of a quality internet connection is an issue. However, today's entrepreneur is resourceful and can bend to her circumstances, and as a result startups are flourishing in developed and developing nations alike. The choice of venue is as individual as you are.

Why I chose to work from home

My road to starting up at home actually started with a phone call from the school principal. My autistic son had just started grade one but was struggling to contain his boundless energy. He needed to go outside and climb things every 15 minutes, but the school thought he needed to be in a tiny curtained off space at the back of the classroom instead. After a month of that, he started throwing himself on the ground and shutting his eyes in protest, and that's when I came home to find five messages on my answering machine, asking me to pick up my child. I arrived at the school office to find my five year old sitting alone in the waiting room while everyone hurried on with their day.

The next day, we were invited in for a chat with the principal, who suggested that maybe we send him to school for only two hours a day. That was the final straw.

In that moment, I knew he was never going to fit with school and was appalled that they would so readily discriminate against my beautiful child. So, we decided to home educate.

Obviously, going to work in an office or opening up a retail space was not going to be an option at that point, so I knew I would have to work from a home base, for the long term.

The amazing thing is, having the kids around 24/7 has not hindered my business in any way. If anything, they've breathed life into it, by giving me room to rediscover my passions. The kids were really excited when I had to run off to a birth in the middle of the night and often came to postnatal visits with me so they could hold the babies.

When we're out and about at activities and visits to the park, my iPad and iPhone come too. I actually had my first booking for a postnatal package while I was setting up a tent on a North Queensland beach. Tent pole in one hand and phone in the other, I took a booking for a $1000 package on the spot. Easy!

Working from home or on the road has not been without its challenges, such as noisy kids walking in on meetings, or screaming at each other when I'm on an important phone call. The logistics of finding last minute babysitters for births, when my husband was out of town on business trips, elevated my stress levels somewhat. Keeping on top of 'Mount Foldmore', my personal laundry mountain, as well as running mum's taxi service for soccer, basketball and scouts while taking calls from clients in the car, is no easy feat. It's even harder when you're a single parent (which I am presently).

Overall though, working from home has been a huge blessing and even if I could work from an office, I'm not sure that I would want to.

Un-Career Story

Sometimes your brilliant un-career can be sparked by a redundancy. Natalie Souprounovich went from redundancy to business owner.

Natalie's Story

I am a senior level designer with 15 years' experience. My passion is designing creative and effective visual communications pieces and graphics for small businesses.

I had been thinking about starting my own business for a few years, but after being made redundant it seemed like it was meant to be. Now I am very excited to be helping small businesses achieve their dream brands.

I love working with businesses that share my passion for creating a clear, consistent message. Whether it is a simple business card or a completely new brand design, I love to see the excitement each client shows when they are presented with their new design.

I usually work when my kids are sleeping, otherwise I find that they are climbing over me and pressing buttons on the keyboard. Sometimes it means late nights, but I have been blessed with children that like to sleep in, so I can usually catch up on the lack of sleep in the morning.

Natalie Souprounovich from Natalie Souprounovich Design Services lives in Brisbane, Queensland, Australia.

Some statistics on the global home-based startup boom

Considering the boom in startups over the past few years, it has actually been really hard to find up-to-date statistics on home-based businesses. However I did discover that currently more than a million Australians work from home (Commonwealth Government of Australia: Small Business website).

According to the latest US Small Business Administration statistics, 52% of all small businesses in America operate from a home base. Small and medium enterprises account for two thirds of all employment in OECD nations. In the UK and Canada, approximately nine percent of businesses are home based.

So on the surface, it appears that small business startups are thriving, but appearances can be deceiving. The reality is that relatively few will make a profit or turn into long term and scalable ventures. US census data shows that more than 50% of new businesses are no longer operating after five years. The percentage of business failures seems to have worsened in the past few years, indicating a great need for support in this industry sector.

Women-owned enterprises are growing in number and are starting to have an impact on economic turnover, according to the latest report by Amex Open Forum on *The State of Women Owned Businesses 2013 (US-based)*. However, male-owned ventures still represent the lion's share of high growth companies.

Entrepreneurship is trending on a global scale and there are many enterprises being kicked off from a home base. Some can be easily scaled while many cannot. But really, does it matter? So long as you are happy at the end of the day, who cares? It's okay to have a solo business that makes enough income to live on but doesn't scale into something bigger. Conversely, it's also okay to start something with a view to growing it into something huge. You choose! It's your life. Don't place artificial limits on what you can achieve.

> This is the generation of empowerment. No longer do you need to be told by someone else whether you are good enough.

This is the generation of empowerment. No longer do you need to be told by someone else whether you are good enough. You know you are and you are going after what you want out of life.

Un-Career Story

Agimary Joseph shares her story of how she made the leap from one country to another.

Agimary's story

I am Agimary, a homeopath from India, with 14 years of experience plus a Bachelor of Homeopathic Medicine and Surgery (B.H.M.S.). I moved to Brisbane in 2009 with my family of two happy healthy boys and my loving husband Joseph. I am working from home to provide both in-clinic and distant consultations.

I studied B.H.M.S. in India where homeopaths are medically trained like a general practitioner, and considered equal to them. I practised homoeopathy in India for ten years before I moved to Australia. Here in Australia, homeopathy is not as popular. I started my practice by renting a place, but I struggled a lot in all aspects; paying the rent, time, transportation etc. I could not find enough time to look after my kids. I have been practising from home for three years now, and am getting enough time and money for my family.

Working from home gives me peace of mind and enough time for my family. I love this place and the people.

Agimary Joseph from Holistic Homeopathy
holistichomeopathy.com.au lives in Brisbane, Queensland, Australia.

Why start up at home?

One thing I've noticed since starting up my business is that the older paradigm, where professionals try to hide the fact they work from home through virtual offices and 1800 numbers, is shifting. Working from home has become the norm for many people, so these days very few try to hide the fact that's where the office is.

A huge sign of this paradigm shift is the grassroots work at home, solopreneur or micro business movement. There are thriving online communities dedicated to supporting people who want to start their own business from a home base.

When you're an entrepreneur or solo business owner operating in such a tough economic climate, it makes sense to work from home where your overheads are lower.

There are many benefits to running a business from home. Achieving a better balance between work and family commitments is one of the primary reasons people choose to work from home.

Other reasons include:

- greater independence
- a more fulfilling work life
- lower establishment and operating costs
- greater flexibility
- convenience of living, working and playing in the one community
- decreased stress

Overall, people tend to choose working from home for intrinsic reasons over extrinsic reasons such as financial gain.

Un-Career Story

In this story, Janine Evans shares how she turned a hobby into a thriving online business.

Janine's Story

My name is Janine. I am a wife and mother of two gorgeous girls who love any type of craft. I took sewing lessons when I was 13 at the local Just Knits store and completed many cross stitch pictures. About nine years ago, when I had trouble finding nice clips and accessories for my hair, I began to make my own Swarovski Crystal clips. Not long after, I began making bows out of grosgrain ribbon.

After my eldest daughter was born I did not return to work. I wanted to stay home with my children. Being a crafty person, I was always making something. At that time I was making beaded items, but like all crafters I made more than I could use myself, so started to sell different things on ebay. This led into party plans and markets. I never really tried to start a business, it's just a hobby that continues to grow.

This business gives me the best of both worlds. I can continue doing what I love while talking to other crafters. I love sourcing new supplies and being able to bring them to my customers, some of whom have now become my friends.

I find being a work-at-home mum can be very difficult. You have to learn to say no to people continuously wanting you to donate your time. Some think that because you are at home you don't have anything to do. Thankfully, that perception is changing.

I love having the opportunity to move work around so I can attend school events or take my children to after school activities. If that means I have to work late because I spent the day at the school tuckshop or running the school's Mother's and Father's days stalls, then that is what I do.

Janine Evans from Sarah Lauren sarahlauren.com.au
lives in Brisbane, Queensland, Australia.

Alternatives to the home office

Even if you base yourself at home, there will be times when you want to work outside the home. The following is a list of alternatives you may want to explore.

Cafés

Meeting clients at a café, or the Coffice as it is now termed, can be a great solution if you have small children at home and toys strewn across the floor most of the day. Cafés can also be good for a change of scene. When I feel I need a creative boost I like to work on my laptop in a café. There's something about a change in energy that can refresh the mind, body and spirit. I also like to use cafés for meeting with new clients, or when it is inconvenient for clients to travel to my home. Some cafés even offer meeting rooms for private meetings and long lunches with clients. Some offer power outlets and wifi too.

Libraries

Many libraries offer free wifi and a variety of resources and services that are helpful for you as a small business owner. Gone are the days when libraries were all about borrowing dog-eared books. There are often free meeting rooms, which are a good alternative for the occasional small group meeting. Some libraries also have larger conference rooms you can hire out. These rooms often have set time limits, so you'll need to talk to your local library to find out what their terms and conditions are.

Serviced offices

Serviced offices are a good solution if you need meeting rooms or a quiet working space more regularly. If you are looking for a casual solution on a regular basis, they may be a good option for you. Serviced offices usually include meeting rooms, internet access, secretarial support and office equipment. Serviced offices offer you the water cooler moments that a normal workplace would have, but the difference is that virtually everyone in the serviced office works for themselves and not for a boss. This means you can enjoy the company and camaraderie without the office politics.

Work hubs, co-working spaces and co-ops

Co-working hubs have sprung from the entrepreneurial boom. They are cooperatively-run facilities for entrepreneurs, home-based business owners and freelancers. Similar to serviced offices, work hubs can offer a variety of equipment, meeting rooms and often internet facilities for people who only need the space on a casual basis. Work hubs are already popular in the UK and US and are just catching on in Australia. They're a great, cheap solution for micro business owners and startup entrepreneurs but they don't offer the range of additional secretarial services that serviced offices do.

Types of businesses you can run from home

The words 'home-based business' have been negatively associated with scams and dodgy Multi Level Marketing schemes in the past, but as more and more legitimate business people set up shop at home, this perception is slowly changing. Following is a summary of some of the more common home-based business types, as well as some pros and cons you may want to consider.

> There needs to be initiatives that nurture women's entrepreneurship in areas typically dominated by men.

Enterprise

By far, the majority of home-based businesses are micro business enterprises covering a range of industries including creative designers, tech startups, service-based businesses, corporate consultants and more. An area where women are not excelling at the same rate as men is information technology, and yet this is a high growth industry. Studies show that one of the reasons for this is that fewer women are pursuing careers in technology than men. If this is to change, there need to be initiatives that nurture women's entrepreneurship in areas typically dominated by men.

Facebook Chief Operations Officer (COO) Sheryl Sandberg has devoted an entire book to this topic. If you don't have *Lean In* on your 'must read' list, jump onto Amazon and download it now!

Food for thought

- Time management skills will be essential. Consider how well you balance the temptation to throw yourself into your project with how much time you spend with your loved ones

- You often end up putting a lot more hours into your business in the initial stages than you get paid for, but over time, this improves as your business grows

- Be careful not to ignore building systems and processes into your business week

- Remember to pay yourself, rather than reinvesting everything in your business. Your time is valuable, so value it!

- You may want to investigate getting a venture capitalist or angel funders on board to fund your project

- You may find you need a mentor to help you focus and grow your business, so you can avoid rookie mistakes and get the right advice from the outset

- Your idea may not take off. Iterate or do something else. It's not failure. You've just learned what doesn't work

Franchise

There are several franchises that can be operated from a home office. These include, but are not limited to, carpet cleaners, domestic cleaners, hairdressers, pest inspectors, building inspectors, builders, accountants, taxation specialists, coffee van vendors, caterers and more. If you're interested in running a franchise, there is information available on organisational and government websites.

Food for thought

- Everything is laid out for you, including training and marketing

- You have the support of a head office if you need advice

- You will be working within the framework of a large corporation and must adhere to their franchise licensing agreements

- Buying a franchise can be an expensive exercise initially, however the return on investment is often a safer bet than starting a business from scratch

Party plan and (legitimate) direct selling businesses

Another really popular option is to run a party plan business. Party plan is when you sell products directly at a social event. Back in the day, Tupperware was the only party plan business I was aware of but, in the past ten years, party plan businesses have exploded and nowadays you can sell anything from jewellery and homewares to health products. There are even enterprising business owners who are setting up party plan businesses from scratch, rather than buying into big corporations.

Food for thought

- To get started, you'll be reliant on people you know to host parties and recommend you to friends

- Often, the time you put into it is a lot more than the financial reward you get out of it, at least initially

- You buy party plan kits up front. Sometimes these don't cost much but sometimes they can be quite expensive

- Party plan can be difficult if you have young children as it often involves a lot of weekend work

- If you find something you love to sell, party plan could be a great option for someone who is a 'people person'

- It pays to do your research and attend some parties as a guest first!

Un-Career Story

Direct selling has proven to be a lucrative business for Dhea Bartlett.

Dhea's Story

I am a mother of three grown up children and teens, happily married for over 23 years. I successfully run my own direct selling business. Knowing that I can build a business of real leveraged residual income inspires me. It's work that I can do once and be paid for over and over. This motivates me because then I can do things with my family, stay at home with my children rather than putting them into child care, and have at least one parent attend all their activities. I am truly grateful for the direct selling industry. What keeps me going is to be able to take trips with my family when we want to, and to enjoy great food and experiences because we can.

The best way for me to market my business is to build relationships. People buy from those they know, like and trust and I invest time and energy in getting to know people through running and attending networking events. I LOVE connecting with people and connecting people with each other.

The biggest challenge for me is staying motivated. I am really good at doing something consistently over time. Massive action bursts I am not good at. I procrastinate like the next person, and I know I spend too much time on social media when I am avoiding the big stuff.

Juggling priorities requires a great deal of organisation. I always put in the non-negotiables for family commitments and then my work fits in around them. We all have the same amount of time. It's what we choose to do with it that matters. If you know your *why – why* you are doing this, you will jump obstacles when they arise and you will push through rejections. Knowing your *why* will help you keep going when others crumble.

If you're establishing your own business, research and dabble in your chosen field while still working. See if you can reduce your corporate workload to fewer hours. Build your business up to a point where you can say goodbye to the corporate world.

Dhea Bartlett from Dhea's ideas sendoutcards.com/dhea lives in Melbourne, Victoria, Australia.

Telecommuting

Quite a few large corporations and universities have provisions for employees wanting to work from home. Telecommuting usually means that you work some hours in the office and some at home. This allows for greater flexibility, especially for mums with young families who want to go back to work. It works for the companies too, as they are able to keep their employees. Replacing staff is an expensive and time-consuming process, so it makes sense to provide for the needs of those employees you don't want to lose. If you're not quite ready to take the leap to solo business ownership or you want to keep a finger in each pie while you get your own enterprise started, this may be an option for you.

Food for thought

- Your company may require you to have your home audited for health and safety standards as you are 'at a workplace' and therefore covered by their policies. If you are employed and wish to remain so as a telecommuter, check to see if your employer supports telecommuting

- You are a direct employee and so are still bound by the company's employment conditions and practises

- You have a measure of flexibility without having to take the investment risk that comes from starting up a franchise, freelance, network marketing business or enterprise

- You get sick leave, recreation leave and employer superannuation

Virtual assistant

Virtual assistants (VAs) provide administrative and secretarial support to businesses. They often specialise in one particular area such as social media management or customer relationship management, appointment setting or website management. A highly skilled virtual assistant is worth his or her weight in gold. While there are companies that offer this service quite inexpensively offshore, there are many opportunities for virtual executive assistants and specialist VAs to promote their skills on a local level. Often offshore VAs require the supervision of a more skilled VA who understands your culture. If you have specialist administration skills, becoming a VA may be just the ticket for you.

Un-Career Story

In this story Hazel Theocharous shares about the flexibility she has as a virtual assistant.

Hazel's Story

I am married with two boys and have worked as a virtual assistant since leaving behind 15 years in the finance, property and legal corporate spheres. When my son first started school, my boss was against me taking leave during school holidays, which became extremely difficult and expensive. I made a decision that was right for me and my family, hence the start of my new career.

Since then I haven't looked back, assisting other small business owners to achieve their own work/life balance. I work on aspects of their business that they either find daunting, do not know how to do or just do not have the time to do.

I love the buzz I get when one of my tips has helped someone, and I love giving back to other business owners. This gives them their time back to concentrate on being at the forefront of their business rather than behind the scenes.

My family and I have recently relocated to London from Sydney, Australia, but I still have a base in Sydney. Most of my marketing is done via social media, email marketing, word of mouth or networking. I love people and I love connecting. I have found that online networking has always worked best to build up a rapport. Then you meet, and the trust factor is already there.

My biggest challenge is the feeling of loneliness or that I am the only one going through the ups and downs of working for myself. However, because of this I can empathise with my clients, and am now an advocate to guide and provide advice to those going through the same things.

At first it can be very daunting to learn to juggle all of the commitments we, as women, have. However, the tried and trusted method I have used, which continues to work, is to work through a weekly calendar before you plan anything extra. Include in it the children's drop off and pick up times, their activities that you need to get them to and then work out what you need to do in your business - allocate time. Remember a bit of flexibility is important, as your business needs change.

Before you leave the corporate world, plan your business. You need to work out where your clients will come from (especially if you have a restraint of trade or something similar). Allow yourself time to prepare for the launch of your business, perhaps even work part time until you leave the corporate world. It is difficult, but if you plan everything out before you leave and start your business, it can be easy.

Hazel Theocharous from Expert VA Global expertvaglobal.com lives in London, UK.

Freelance professional services

If you have coding, website development, accounting, public relations, design experience and more, opportunities abound in the online space. Websites such as elance.com and odesk.com regularly advertise freelance opportunities. Chances are that you will find just the opportunity for you.

Food for thought

- Most freelancers bid for work and freelance websites such as odesk.com and elance.com are highly competitive. Focus on the skills you bring to the table and the value you offer when communicating with potential clients

- Once you've done one freelance contract, it is easier to get more work— getting that first freelance opportunity is the hard part

- Be wary of businesses that don't want to pay you what you're worth. They are looking for a cheap solution, not necessarily a quality one

- Keep in mind that businesses looking for freelancers do not want the added expense of an employee with on-costs. So make sure your rates are market rates. You are saving the company thousands by sub-contracting to them

- Don't promise what you can't deliver. Over-delivering is better than not delivering a quality product or service

Un-Career Story

Freelancing can be a brilliant for the person who wants to work for themselves but it has it's challenges, as explained by Nicole Leedham.

Nicole's Story

My business is freelance writing - copywriting, corporate documents, web content etc. I work mainly with small and medium-sized business clients, including academic clients and membership organisations. I help them by writing things they either don't have the time or the skills to do, such as annual reports, press releases, SEO web copy, flyers, newsletters etc. I have both a marketing and PR background that I bring to my work, so I'm not just writing in a vacuum.

I had always wanted to freelance, but never had the courage. When my dad died, just eight weeks after my second child was born, I realised there were no second chances. I started to put the wheels in motion, and resigned from work about two and a half years later. The catalyst on the day I resigned was my boss basically telling me that my skills were redundant because they could just get interstate material and rebrand it. I handed in my notice on my way out of the office that very day. I still do pretty much what I have always done in a job, but now I have clients that appreciate me.

I love what I do. I have no intention of going back to working for someone else. The variety is great, my clients are (mostly) awesome, and I am my own boss. Sure, there are some times when it's hard to get motivated and some topics I have to write about are not exactly scintillating, but the fact that I need to feed the family gets me off the couch and in front of the 'puter.

My biggest challenge is time management. There is always someone or something that wants a piece of me. When I am with the kids, I feel I am neglecting the business, and vice versa.

I market my business via social media-Facebook, Google+ and LinkedIn mainly, but the ROI on them is not great, to be honest. The best marketing I have done is get off my backside and network with people in person. I made sure I invested in a quality logo, business cards, website etc. to ensure the business looked professional right from the start. I get most of my clients from referrals, word-of-mouth and repeat business, and I have a few ongoing relationships that provide a nice base income, while they last.

Being honest, juggling work and family is something I don't feel I do very well. I have a winemaker husband (good planning, right?), a nine-year old son, a five year old daughter and an 81-year old widowed mum who lives independently, but as an only child, I feel responsible for her.

I used to think it was all the distractions in the office that were a problem, but now I realise I am easily distracted. I try not to work on weekends unless absolutely necessary. I know all the time management hints and tips, I am just lousy at implementing them.

If you're considering leaving a full time job to start your own business, my suggestion would be to make sure you have six months to a year of savings. It took about 18 months for my networking etc. to start paying dividends and for me to feel that this thing actually had legs. In hindsight, perhaps I should have stayed at work a little longer and put up with the fact I was rebranding interstate material! Thankfully, we had some savings, and at least one regular income. This year, it looks as if my freelancing income will outstrip that regular PAYE income! Cheers to that!

Nicole Leedham from Black Coffee Communication
blackcoffeecommunication.com.au lives in Adelaide,
South Australia, Australia.

So many choices

Whatever path you take, there are bound to be challenges along the way, but the benefits can be enormous as well. It really is about finding the opportunity that works for you and going for it.

You may be wondering what choices are right for you when it comes to where to base your business. The great news is that you can change your mind at any point. If working from home is not working for you, you can look into co-working spaces. If freelancing is not working for you, you can change course and try your hand at something else. Don't limit yourself to just one option. You may even find a few options may be your cup of tea. For instance, I know plenty of people who run party plan businesses in addition to freelancing and telecommuting. Do what works for you!

Action Step

Take 20 minutes to jot down the pros and cons of working from home as opposed to working in a co-working space or serviced office.

Are you suited to working from a home base?

How well do you cope with distractions?

Is your internet sufficient to run online programs?

If you are not clear on your *why*, take a few minutes to think about what kind of work you enjoy and what appeals to you from the ideas you've been reading about.

Bonus: Download bonus resources that dig deeper into this topic. For this chapter, I interviewed Matthew Dunstan, author of The *Co-Working Revolution, 4 steps to creating a more successful home enterprise*. There's also a free Where to Base Your Business worksheet to help you figure out if working from home (or somewhere else) is for you and a printable affirmation to inspire you to take action now. To access these bonus resources, simply sign up here: bit.ly/uncareerresources

Chapter 6

How to get clear on your branding

Your branding is how you present yourself, from your imagery and colours to your fonts and the way you write. A brand is not just a name and a logo. Business names and logos are by-products of branding; they support the message you want to convey. I love Virgin Airlines' branding. It permeates every aspect of the business. Even the driest business letters are spruced up with a little bit of fun, because that's the image Virgin aims to portray: 'We are super-fun, and when you travel with us, you'll have a blast and we might even do some face-painting!'

When I started my first business venture, I was a bit all over the place. I had a terrific logo and a great tagline but had my fingers in a lot of different pies. I wanted to combine all my interests into the one business, which meant a retail arm with my homemade accessories and homewares, as well as my birth doula service and postnatal service. When people asked me what I did, I found it really hard to give a clear answer. I'd say "Well, I attend births and cook meals for families afterwards and sew handmade products, oh and help with breastfeeding…" It was really confusing, not only for me but for my clients.

I learned from that, and went on to streamline Mumatopia. I rebranded so I could be really clear about what I offered. In the end I reduced the retail arm to just products related to mothers and babies and focused on my birth and postnatal services. Now that my focus has shifted to my marketing business, Mumatopia has become more of a personal blog, so another rebrand may well be on the cards in the near future.

Being clear on what it is you offer and why is important to the conversion process. If you confuse potential clients, they are unlikely to purchase from you, so you need to make the path easy to follow. In order to do this effectively, it helps to identify who exactly you are talking to and why, then add in a touch of who you are for authenticity. Once you have worked that out, deciding what logo, colours and language to use becomes a whole lot easier!

If you're worried about getting it wrong, remember that branding changes over time, as does your business. You have to start somewhere. Almost every large, long-term business I know of has gone through a process of branding and rebranding. So don't get too hung up on the choices you make now. You can always change them down the track, and you probably will.

Developing effective branding

I recently treated my three boys to lunch at the food court in a local shopping centre. Not being one to pass up an opportunity to teach them something about the world, I gave them a conundrum to solve.

Amongst the array of outlets in the food court there was one that had no customers. It was relatively new to the food court, and as I sat there, puzzling over why people were passing it by, I put the question to my boys: "Why do you think no one is buying from that new hamburger shop??"

These were our collective observations:
"McDonalds is two shops down, Mum."
"There's too many words."
"They use the word 'real' a little too much."
"There's no big pictures of juicy burgers."
"They're not fun enough."
"Their colour scheme is dull compared to the other shops." (they all featured primary colours in their branding)
"Their main colour looks like spew." (it was actually mustard)

Okay, I could go on, but you get the picture.

While I could see what this outlet was trying to achieve with its vintage-coloured branding, it wasn't working. A lot of it boiled down to the colour scheme, but also it simply didn't fit with a food court primarily aimed at families and young people.

Even the dodgy sandwich joint was getting orders over this neat and clean operation.

It's true that there could have been other factors at play for this food outlet. Their burgers may have failed to live up to the wordy promises on their noticeboard. Their pricing could have also been a factor. However, watching the sad performance of this outlet was a lesson on how important branding is to the success of a small business.

So, what are the two most important considerations when it comes to branding your small business or budding enterprise?

1. Your Ideal Client

Your branding is more about your ideal customer than it is about you. Yes, you need your personality reflected in your brand but it should reflect your ideal customers so that you can attract the right people to your business.

One of the biggest mistakes new businesses make is to try to reach a broad range of people. The thing is though, if you're trying to reach everyone, you'll end up appealing to no one.

Potential customers don't want to feel like part of a crowd. They are more likely to be drawn in when you talk to them directly. You can speak clearly to them if you have narrowly defined who it is you most want to talk to. The more you narrow down your target audience, the easier it will be for you to establish branding that appeals to them.

If you can define who you most want to do business with, you'll still attract others who don't exactly fit your ideal buyer persona, but they'll be attracted to you for the right reasons. These people will likely resonate with the way you communicate, with your branding and with your services. Those people who identify with how you do business will be attracted to you, regardless of whether they're an exact fit or not.

To define your ideal client, it helps to build a profile of a person that you most want to work with. You do this by determining their demographic profile, their psychographic profile, their motivations, their influencers and mediators. Give them a name and an address, hobbies, dreams and struggles. This then informs your branding. It's not just about creating a buyer persona based on who is buying from you now. They may very well be the wrong people for your business and end up being problem clients at the end of the day.

It's not an easy exercise because it requires you to zero in on who you ideally want to work with and in what capacity. For businesses that have more than one target market, this can be a tricky process, but once you break through that barrier of trying to appeal to everyone, you will start coming up with brilliant ideas for your branding and marketing.

Case Study: Evans and Evans Pools, ideal client profile

I used this process to work with a local pool builder to create an ideal client profile. It is a picture of a person, not a target market, not a demographic profile, but a person you can imagine in your head. This profile gave them a clear idea of what their branding needed to achieve.

Meet Kylie, a 40 year old mother of two older primary school age kids. Kylie is married to Greg, who works in a city office. Kylie is a part time receptionist at the local vet. They live in their own house in the suburbs on a reasonably large block. They've been building their equity for a few years so they have some cash to play with.

Kylie likes fairly low key family activities. They don't travel a lot and prefer simple pleasures like lazing around the house, gardening and camping.

Kylie has an iPhone and her kids have iPads.

She is not particularly religious and values family time above most other things.

Kylie is struggling to find time for family, quality of life, quality time with Greg, how to bring the family together for shared experiences and memories, extended family responsibilities. She's starting to think about retiring in 15 years and wants to improve her home's saleability and market appeal for the future. She likes a hassle-free life, so she's looking for easy solutions.

She is a soccer mum and is actively involved in sporting groups.

Kylie's extended family, friends and media are quite influential. She admires underdogs who've made it big, people like JK Rowling and sporting heroes, as well as people who've overcome adversity.

Online, Kylie is mainly hanging out on Facebook to socialise with friends and family. She also belongs to a couple of groups including one on eczema and allergies (one of her kids has eczema) and one for local mums from her local school.

Kylie also enjoys Pinterest and Instagram to find home and lifestyle ideas, recipes and inspiration.

She follows popular blogs such as www.mamamia.com.au and mainstream news websites but she also reads up on allergy blogs.

For information on local products, services and activities she is researching she mainly goes to Facebook, Brisbane Kids and Kidspot.

Kylie is considering building a pool as it may:

Meet needs to increase quality of life and time for family fun at home

Keep growing kids home for fun—social hub

Be easy to maintain and care for

Improve value/saleability of home

Be there all year round for enjoyment, doesn't require a special trip away.

Kylie's questions about pools may include:

How long does it take to build a pool?

How much is it?

What are some of the additional/hidden costs I should be aware of?

What are the legal requirements?

Can we do our own design?

Will it improve the value of our home?

Where's the best place to put a pool?

What's the payment schedule?

What kind of pool is right for my family?

What are the health benefits of a magnesium salt pool?

What type of pool is best for kids with allergies?

Should I put in a spa?

Is it worth heating my pool?

What's the process for putting the pool in?

Can I afford a pool?

Should I build my own pool?

Does pool concrete crack?

Is a pool safe during a bushfire?

Evans and Evans Pools' brand imagery

Because they now understand what their ideal client, Kylie, is looking for, Evans and Evans Pools' brand imagery hones in on family fun. The design they chose was light-hearted and a bit cheeky. They moved away from the traditional pool website colour scheme of primary blues and greens so that they'd stand out from the other pool builder brands.

Evans and Evans Pools' social media platforms

Evans and Evans Pools currently focus their online marketing on Pinterest and Facebook. They are yet to delve into Instagram but that will come as they get used to the tools available to them. They have the most success and engagement when they post pictures of pools they are currently building. Analytical tools on social media show that their primary audience is women within the same age bracket and demographic profile as Kylie.

Evans and Evans Pools' blog

Evans and Evans Pools' blog focuses on answering Kylie's key questions about building a pool. This blog is a work in progress but so far, it's honed in on the needs that Kylie has identified.

There is enormous value in carefully defining your ideal client profile. It not only helps you visualise your potential clients but it also helps you develop content ideas that will help to meet their needs and address gaps in the marketplace that your competitors may not be meeting. In Evans and Evans Pools' case, there were virtually no other local pool builders developing a strong presence on Pinterest at the time. Images from the Evans and Evans Pools' Pinterest boards have been shared across Pinterest virally, drawing more people to their social presence and more people to their website.

Results

Over the course of a year and a half, the results have been quite dramatic. Evans and Evans Pools went from spending $15,000 a year on mainstream advertising with no return on investment, to less than $5,000 a year on a minimalist content and social media strategy. Their new branding and marketing has started to pay off. It has resulted in increased traffic to the website and increased referrals. The business has reported that it is having its busiest winter season ever. When they have asked buyers where they found the company, the answer has consistently been Facebook and the website.

The strategy we put in place was quite minimal, as the company was not prepared to make a heavy investment in social media and content until it yielded proven results. This is not a strategy I usually recommend. Content is an investment and it should be taken seriously, especially when traditional ads aren't resulting in return on investment. However, it also goes to show that even a minimalist strategy can yield great results.

Action Steps

Take a few minutes to assess your current branding. Does your branding attract the right people to your business, or like the burger joint, does it sit as a less appealing option amongst a pool of competitors?

Brainstorm some ideas on what your ideal client might look like. Think about what he or she might be interested in and what questions he or she might have in relation to the products or services you offer.

Focus on how you are serving your ideal customer or client. What will they get out of your product or service? How does it meet their needs?

2. Your brand personality and story

Your unique brand personality and story is the second important consideration. Your story is your reason for starting up, your motivations and your unique perspective. Inject your personality into your brand so that you can present an authentic image to your ideal clients.

An important question to ask prior to developing your brand is: "Who am I?"

If your business was a person, what would he or she look like? Who would he or she hang out with? What's his or her vibe? The answers will tell you a lot about the direction you should develop your branding in.

It's important that your brand has an authenticity to it. If you are a super-serious person, having a brand that is fun and flowery probably won't work for you. The moment someone meets you they'll see the incongruity between how you behave and how you represent yourself in your branding materials and online presence.

If your branding is in alignment with who you are, then it will be easier for your potential clients to trust that what you say is true.

Action Step

Have a think about your personality and characteristics. How can you authentically reflect these in your branding?

Choosing a business name

Names are important, as they define your business style and your business type. One of the first things you'll need to do before you can legally register your business is to choose a name. Before deciding on a name, there are a number of things you need to keep in mind. Here are some of the more important ones:

Consider your ideal client

When you're brainstorming ideas for your business name, take into account your ideal client's expectations of your brand. For example, if your ideal client is interested in high end couture fashion, you wouldn't use a cute business name. You would aim for something sophisticated.

Consider your brand personality

Is your brand serious and formal, or informal and fun? Is your brand mainstream or alternative? It's important to choose a name that adequately reflects the personality of your brand.

Is your chosen name available?

When you're brainstorming, narrow it down to a few favourites. Your top choice may not be available. There are business name search tools you can use in most English speaking countries to help you find out if your chosen name has already been taken by someone else. You can usually find these tools on government websites.

Can you secure the domain name?

One of the most important things you can do to establish your brand is to set up your own website and domain name. Domain names are quite inexpensive and by adding your domain name to all promotional materials, you extend the reach of your brand. If you want to appeal to a local audience, make sure you also secure the local version of your domain name such as .com.au.

Can you trademark the name?

No matter what country you live in, there are rules for trademarking business names. For instance, you cannot trademark a business name that is also a place name. Check with a trademark specialist for information on whether your business name is able to be trademarked.

Where design and brand imagery come in

A well-designed brand is one that seamlessly incorporates your voice and your ideal client's voice. It takes into consideration your prospects' needs and preferences, and effortlessly leads your prospects where they need to go, whether that be on your website, in printed material or on social media. Design architecture is usually separated from branding in the marketing sphere. In reality your branding and marketing don't exist in isolation from each other. Below are some basic tips to help you factor in design elements that will help your brand shine.

> A well-designed brand is one that seamlessly incorporates your voice and your ideal client's voice.

Brand consistency

- Decide on a font and styling and stick with it! A good rule of thumb is to pick two fonts, one for titles and one for body text and subtitles. Try to pick fonts that are easy to read both on and off line. Steer away from overused fonts such as comic sans

- Decide on your brand's colours and stick to them. If you can, use Pantone colour codes for your logo colours and take the time to set up hexidecimal colour conversions in your photo editing program. If you don't know how to do this, get a graphic designer to do it for you and ask them to list your colour palate in various formats:

  - CMYK—Cyan, Magenta, Yellow and Key Black, for four colour offset printing of business cards etc

  - RGB - Red, Green, Blue for online publications

  - Hexidecimal that start with a # with six numbers or letters following. E.g. White is #ffffff. The hexidecimal colour codes will be important when setting up social media pages, blogs and email newsletters

Brand architecture

When designing the layout of social channels and your website, decide what information elements are most important. For instance, which Facebook tabs are most crucial to feature on your Facebook Page? If you are focusing on visual social media, think about themes for boards on Pinterest and hashtags for your Instagram account.

On your website, what are the key menu items your prospects will look for to find the information they need? A basic website should contain a 'home' page featuring the most important information about your brand, business or products. In addition, an 'about' page gives viewers behind the scenes information about you as well as some history behind the development of your business. A 'contact' page should feature several ways in which someone can contact you. Another great page to add is a 'testimonials' page. People like to read testimonials from other clients and customers who have done business with you, as it reassures them that you are legitimate and customer-focused.

Brand images

A professionally designed logo can be a real asset. You can easily resize it for different mediums and trademark it. If you have graphic design skills you can most likely come up with a decent set of graphics yourself using Adobe Illustrator, Photoshop or similar. There are also free graphic programs online such as canva.com. However, many small business operators enlist a professional graphic designer to design a logo and business identity for their businesses. It does not have to be an expensive exercise. There are many graphic designers who work from home and have fantastic rates because of their low overheads. To prepare, start by taking these steps:

- Draw a concept for a logo yourself, scan it and then engage a graphic designer to turn it into a finished vector graphic in Adobe Illustrator or similar. It will cost you less and you'll be able to use your logo image on all products you create, including printed materials such as business cards, T-shirts, hats and mugs

- Use fiverr.com or 99designs.com to help you come up with a basic conceptual design and then take that to a professional logo designer to do the finished artwork. Again, it's a lot cheaper and, so long as your logo is original and uses no graphic elements from stock image libraries, you'll be able to trademark it

Choosing a logo designer

Finding the right designer to take your business concept and turn it into a logo can be hard when you don't know where to start looking. Prices vary a great deal, so it's a good idea to thoroughly check out a designer before engaging them to work with you.

Where to find designers

You can find graphic designers via fiverr.com, if you are bootstrapping it. If you would prefer to work with a local designer you can meet up with in person, there are a number of online directories that feature graphic designers. It's also a good idea to ask business colleagues for referrals.

When you are interviewing a designer:

- Check out the designer's website. Does it reflect the image they've portrayed as a designer? Does it showcase their recent work? Is there more information detailing their background and experience?

- Check out the designer's portfolio. A good designer will have a lot of examples of their work on display on their website. A portfolio that includes the names of companies and businesses they've designed for as well as examples is a sign that they mean business

- Ask the designer if they use images downloaded from a stock photo library. If they do, but they don't spell that out in their communication with you, then you might want to look elsewhere. It's okay to use stock imagery if those images are licensed for commercial use. The same applies to fonts. However, you cannot trademark a logo that uses stock images. Note: be sure to check the licensing agreement before using a stock image. Different platforms have different agreements in place

- If you are planning on expanding your business beyond a Facebook page, it's important to have a unique logo and branding that you can eventually trademark. If that's the case, engage a designer who is experienced in unique logo design and branding

- Check out the designer's testimonials. If they don't have any on their website, keep a wide berth. If they do, make sure you can check out their work somewhere and even speak to a couple of past clients

- Have a look at the designer's design process. Is it thorough? Is it a step-by-step process?

Getting your story straight

Regardless of what online tools you use, it's a good idea to have a consistent story to share. People like to know who it is they're going to do business with. Don't be afraid to put your face and name to your business to help build trust and credibility.

Create a 90 second pitch to use the next time someone asks you what you do, otherwise known as an elevator pitch. If they don't get it, go back to the drawing board. A good pitch may just open the door to a business opportunity, so it is important to get your words right, both in writing and in person. You can then use your pitch when you introduce yourself, both on and offline.

When you write a tagline or elevator pitch, ensure it screams benefits or outcomes. It's a common mistake for new business people to try to sell based on who they are and how they label themselves, rather than what's in it for the customer. A terrific model for elevator pitches is the Gaddie Pitch.

In a Gaddie Pitch, named after creator Antony Gaddie, you paint a picture for the person you are talking to. First you introduce the problem with the words, "You know how..."

E.g. "You know how small businesses jump onto social networks without much of a plan, just a bit here and there, and then wonder why they aren't attracting customers?"

Next you say how you solve the problem and provide key benefits and outcomes, using the lead in, "What we do is..."

E.g. "What we do is help small business owners identify the gaps in their marketing and then fill in the potholes and work towards a systematic approach to their marketing. This helps them save time, money and hassle because their marketing is more focused and they aren't wasting time on people who will never buy from them."

Next you present a case study with the final lead in, "In fact..."

E.g. "In fact, a recent client of mine, XYZ, is now getting regular enquiries as a result of putting this system into place. They are spending less time on social media for more gain."

The beauty of this model is that you don't sound like you're selling anything. Instead you're telling a story about what you do as a business to solve people's problems. Done well, this can be very powerful.

You can find out more about the Gaddie Pitch at the Gaddie Pitch Training Centre on the Anthill website: anthillonline.com/gaddie-pitch-training-centre.

Action Steps

Use these three questions to help you develop your pitch.

- What is the problem that you address?

- How do you help your clients address this problem?

- What's an example you give of a client that has had results by working with you?

Bonus: Download bonus resources that dig deeper into this topic. For this chapter, I interviewed Annemarie Cross, award winning business and branding coach and presenter of The Ambitious Entrepreneur podcast. There's also a free Branding Checklist and a printable affirmation to inspire you to take action now. To access these bonus resources, simply sign up here: bit.ly/uncareerresources

Chapter 7

Marketing your business, 21st Century style!

For your business to thrive in a competitive market, it pays to set yourself apart. But how do you establish yourself as the go-to person in your niche? How do you create memorable brand experiences that entice and compel your ideal clients to want to know more?

If your plan is to throw a few strategies together and hope they work, what is commonly called the spray and pray approach, then I'm really glad you got your hands on this book. In the following pages, I'm going to share with you how to build a marketing system that attracts genuine clients to your business and social media profiles, and saves you time, money and hassle. A good marketing system breathes life into your marketing and feeds the lead generation cycle.

This is the system I use in my own marketing as well as my clients'. It helps identify gaps in your marketing and put strategies in place to attract genuine potential clients.

Marketing ain't marketing anymore!

Marketing and customer service are more entwined than ever before.

In marketing, we used to talk about marketing messages and getting our messages 'out there'. Not any more. Marketing has changed. In fact, I'm not even sure we should call it marketing anymore, but rather communication and conversation. A Nielsen study in 2012 found that consumers were hyper-informed about brands and products. They do their research before they make contact, using social media to find more information about brands, check out reviews from other consumers and compare products and pricing.

Consumers are highly attuned to marketing-speak and 'salesy' sales people, and they are turned off big time when businesses use this approach. These days, consumers need to know you, then like you, before they can begin to trust you. It's only then that they will consider buying from you. It's this 'know, like, trust' factor that is integral to the new way of marketing. A terrific book to read more about developing the 'know, like, trust' factor is Guy Kawasaki's *Enchantment*.

Consumers are researchers

Consumers are doing more research than ever before and are often introduced to a new product or service via their friends and contacts on social media. This research is not limited to big ticket items like houses and cars. People are researching everything, from kids clothing to where to go out for dinner on the weekend.

Thanks to smartphones, customers can now compare prices and find product reviews on the spot, in the shop. It certainly saves a lot of legwork! That means the onus is on businesses to demonstrate their value to potential customers as never before. As a result, content marketing, where you use content to educate and inform consumers to make informed buying decisions, is accounting for larger proportions of marketing budgets.

Forget campaigns - go for consistency

Social media is not a one-way medium and that means marketing is no longer about campaigns and brand messages. Businesses are using social media to interact directly with their consumers on a daily basis. As a result of the shift in the way businesses communicate with their followers on social media, marketing has become less about creating specific campaigns than it has about consistently communicating and interacting with potential clients. Social media makes it possible to get instant feedback on products and services and consumers expect brands to be responsive.

Potential customers want to find product information on their own terms. When they ask a question, they expect a prompt reply. Businesses need to be prepared to be a part of the conversation. Marketing and customer service are more entwined than ever before.

> Social media enables that word of mouth to spread faster and further than it would if you simply responded to a friend's email or phone call.

Consumers talk about you, for better or worse

Social media is amplifying word of mouth like never before. Instead of attempting to recall a product recommendation that came up over coffee with friends, we're now doing a search on Facebook and Google for the conversation thread. Every conversation is able to be archived and retrieved. Many small businesses rely on word of mouth referrals to drive people their way. Small businesses work hard to ensure their customers are happy, and happy customers help out their friends who are looking for the same services. Social media enables that word of mouth to spread faster and further than it would if you simply responded to a friend's email or phone call. We'll go more in-depth into social media marketing fundamentals a little later on.

These trends show that inbound marketing strategies like blogging, SEO and sharing valuable content on social networks are more important than ever before. If you want to market your products and services, it pays to be a part of the consumer conversation. This means rewiring your mindset to focus outwardly on how you can add value to the consumer experience. Otherwise your potential clients will give you the cold shoulder and your brand will miss out on business.

Consumers don't listen to people they don't know

If someone came up to you on the street and starting telling you what you should do and how you should do it, you'd likely run in the opposite direction. However, if your friends recommend something, you're more likely to listen and try out what they are doing.

Influencers are everywhere

Everybody you connect with may not be a customer or client, but they may be an influencer. Whenever you share an article, status update or commentary on social media, your organic reach or visibility on each platform is largely determined by the reach of your followers, likers and connections. If you write a kick-ass blog post and it is shared by people in your networks who are influencers, your reach will be greater than if it's only shared by a family member who's not particularly engaged with the subject matter but wants to share it to be nice.

Why inbound marketing is the new black

Content marketing and inbound marketing are relatively new terms in the marketing sphere, but if you've been burying your head in the sand, it's time to pull it out! Traditional marketing is dead and inbound marketing has buried it!

What is inbound marketing?

Inbound marketing is where you pull people into your business rather than push your business on them. You attract them rather than distract them! You communicate rather than manipulate. To do this, you'll need to focus on a niche rather than broadcast to a crowd.

Inbound marketing is marketing that draws your prospective clients into your sales funnel. It includes:

- search marketing (Search Engine Optimisation)

- content marketing (using self-published and shared content to educate, entertain and build relationships with your potential clients, clients and other stakeholders)

- social media marketing (Facebook marketing, Twitter, Pinterest etc.) and

- permission-based marketing (email marketing to people who subscribe for your updates)

What's happened to traditional marketing?

When I was at university studying communication, the disruptive marketing model was drummed into us. We were taught to find creative ways to grab people's attention and keep them in front of the TV set, or glued to the radio during ad breaks.

84% of people trust the recommendations of people they know on social media.

It's no secret that broadcast media has been struggling. Newspapers, magazines and television stations rely on advertising revenue to make a profit. However, with more readers looking to the internet for news, and the rising dominance of inbound marketing tools, fewer and fewer small businesses are investing in traditional media. Small businesses are not only the backbone of whole economies but of the advertising industry as well.

The Nielsen Global Survey of Trust in Advertising Q1 2013 showed some astonishing figures in relation to consumer behaviour on social media. The study showed that 84% of people trust the recommendations of people they know on social media. What was interesting about this study was that branded websites and consumer opinions online both outstripped mainstream information sources such as news articles, and magazine and TV advertising.

Apart from a clear shift away from traditional advertising, it was surprising that websites and online opinion outstripped news articles. Traditionally, articles

Traditional Marketing

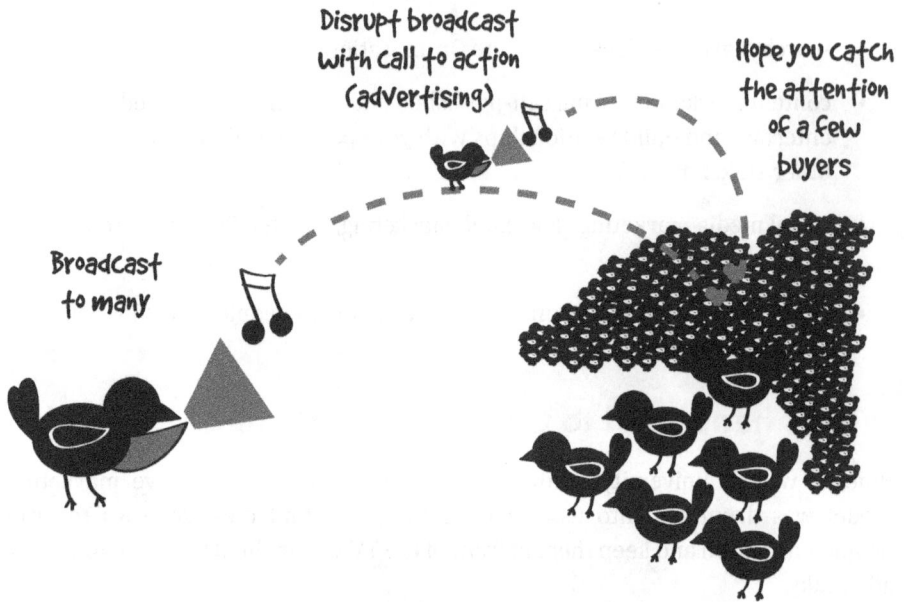

Disrupt broadcast with call to action (advertising)

Hope you catch the attention of a few buyers

Broadcast to many

Inbound Marketing

Expand your following through amplified word of mouth (social media)

Be helpful. Create conversation. Inspire sharing!

Focus on a specific niche

© 2013 Cas McCullough

written by journalists have been seen as more authoritative and trustworthy than many other sources. The biggest takeaway from this study for me was that people's reliance on recommendations, genuine information and word of mouth is growing, and that's why inbound marketing techniques are becoming more and more popular.

Why inbound marketing is gaining more traction with business owners

Inbound marketing has a lower cost per lead than traditional marketing. Social media is largely free to use, and that makes the cost of traditional advertising look rather expensive in comparison.

Many small businesses are feeling the pain of low return on investment (ROI) on broadcast advertising, now that the majority of consumers are using social media and mobile technology to make informed buying decisions.

More sophisticated permission-based marketing software enables small businesses to automate and personalise their marketing to a greater degree than ever before. Not only can you segment people based on their demographics or interests, you can also segment them by their behaviour around specific interests. Rather than focusing on a large crowd, instead, you can focus on a specific niche, on creating conversation, being helpful and leading the right people to make an informed decision about investing in your offering (and in themselves).

Social media enables businesses to narrowcast rather than broadcast. Narrowcasting enables you to reach out to a specific niche, thereby making your advertising and communication more personalised and relevant to your intended audience. Growth occurs as a result of providing value to your niche, creating conversation and amplified word of mouth, which is when people in your niche share, like and interact with your content.

What's stopping small businesses from investing in inbound marketing?

The inbound marketing process takes time, maybe even up to a year or more. Joe Pullizi, dubbed the Godfather of Content Marketing and founder of the Content Marketing Institute, has said that it can take up to three years to build loyalty. However, as most people don't make snap decisions to buy big ticket items, this is okay. In the meantime, you can develop a relationship with followers and subscribers through social media, be helpful and keep sharing valuable content that will help your buyers make informed decisions about investing in your products or services.

Inbound marketing is a long-term strategy, not a short-term fix.

What is stopping small businesses from making the investment is perhaps an unrealistic expectation from the outset. Inbound marketing is a long-term strategy, not a short-term fix. For inbound marketing to work, you need to put your heart into your content, and focus on meeting the needs of specific niches at specific points in the client lifecycle, rather than spreading a wide net, hoping you catch something good. If you want a quick fix, then you'll want to back up your longer-term strategies with some shorter-term, but still highly targeted, advertising campaigns.

Un-Career Story

Mary shares some valuable insights and tips on how to use inbound marketing methods such as content marketing and social media marketing to gain a foothold and establish yourself as an expert in your niche.

Mary's Story

As Quality Supervisor of the government DNA Forensic Lab, I was living a lifelong dream of working in forensics, and this also opened up lecturing opportunities at a local university. As Principal Quality Advisor for the government Radiology Projects team I was making a real difference to health outcomes in communities like the small Western Queensland town I grew up in.

After being in a stressful work situation, I had just landed a fantastic, well-paid position working with a wonderful group of people so I really had no inclination to leave. However, life decided to throw a curve ball and three months after giving birth to my youngest daughter I was told I had melanoma. Thankfully it was in the very early stages and after surgery I was told all should be ok as long as I had three monthly skin checks. Really, I had dodged a bullet but there were times while I was waiting for my pathology results that I was thinking, "What if this is it?" I had a very young family and I still want to do so much. I had always wanted to run my own business and I decided that if ever there was a time to reassess my vision for my and my family's future it was now. Three months later my husband and I started bringing LogiQA to life.

Now I use my experience implementing and maintaining quality management systems to help other small businesses and scientific facilities implement their own systems. This allows them to be more competitive for tenders and contracts both for private industry and government. Using our scientific background, we also provide technical accreditation support to scientific and health facilities.

The biggest challenge I face is being spread too thinly across all the important aspects of my business. It has been a fantastic learning experience though. The other challenge, which I chose, is to build the business part time while I continued to be at home with my young daughters. I'm glad I chose this path but it isn't without a variety of disadvantages. I'm sure the business would be in a much better place if I was available full time, but I'm happy to spend the time with my girls. As the girls grow and head off to school and kindy, I'll get more time to work on the business.

Our drive to make a success from our business keeps my husband and I motivated. Just in case I have a blah moment, I have a vision board above my desk that shows the life I'd like for my family, which usually makes me smile then get back to it. There's nothing like the reality and expense of real life to keep you motivated as well.

In hindsight we really needed more start-up capital, so we've been limited to low cost marketing options. Content marketing is where I've devoted most of my time. I write articles for the LogiQA website and have developed infographics and quizzes as well as conducting interviews with industry experts. I've put together some presentations for Slideshare, am a regular contributor for Flying Solo and have written guest articles for other websites. I use Sourcebottle for other guest writing opportunities.

We have a Facebook page, LinkedIn personal and company page, Google+ personal and company page, Pinterest company page and Twitter company page. While I was initially more comfortable with Facebook, I've had most business success with Twitter. The Twitter chats I participate in have been especially useful for making contacts and finding other great small businesses to work with. The time I've invested learning about and implementing SEO has yielded the most return, with our biggest clients and prospects coming from organic SEO searches.

Offline networking opportunities have been limited due to my availability but I intend to devote more time to this in future. For now, online networking through Twitter and flyingsolo.com.au have been the most beneficial for my business.

It has been difficult juggling the business with the personal commitments of a young family. Most weekends are consumed by meeting business deadlines, though with more time to work on the business this year, I'm hoping to reclaim more family time. If you have specialist skills, if you are a marketing professional, an IT professional etc., make sure you enlist the help of other specialists in the areas that aren't your strength. You can learn to do lots of things, but you get a much bigger head start if you get some professional direction first.

When starting your own business, make sure you have sufficient startup funds, as it's likely to take more time and cost more than you think, especially if you make a mistake or two along the way. Also, remember that however hard you've worked for someone else's business, running your own business is at least twice as hard and more importantly many, many times more satisfying.

*Mary Gardam from LogiQA logiqa.com.au lives in
Brisbane, Queensland, Australia.*

How consumers are using inbound marketing

In order to stand out from the noise on the internet, it pays to meet potential clients where they are in the buying cycle. As part of that, an inbound marketing strategy is essential.

Here's a common scenario:

I am looking for accommodation in Sydney. I ask on my Facebook status: "Can anyone recommend a good 4-star hotel in Sydney?"

Why do I do this first? Because I'd rather get recommendations from people I know, like and trust, or at least from people my friends know, like and trust, than from anywhere else.

At the same time, a Sydney hotel has a Facebook ad campaign running. If my keywords and demographic profile are in the campaign's keyword list, their ad will then show up on my Facebook profile.

What's more, if my friends 'like' the hotel's page, I would be more likely to click on the ad link and check out the hotel. If the page is full of ads, spam and there's little interaction, I'd probably look elsewhere, but if there is good interaction and I can see that the hotel is responding to questions and comments and sharing valuable information, I might 'like' them.

From there, I'd look for a URL on the 'About' section and check out their website. I might then search for reviews on TripAdvisor.com before going back to individual friends to ask more questions.

If the hotel has a brochure-style website with little information on it, I'll bounce back to Facebook or elsewhere pretty quickly. However, if they have lots of well-organised, helpful information, I'll hang around and check it out. I'll then go and look at other suggestions before finally making a decision.

I researched three hotels that my friends recommended, and each had similar pricing and similar features, but one hotel website had articles featuring local activities, events and resources. Which hotel do you think I was drawn to?

The key to marketing these days is to think less about manipulating your audience and more about providing outstanding service. Remember, the object is to make an impression so indelible that you're the first brand to come to mind when a former client is asked for a recommendation. Whether you have a social media presence or not, consumers are talking about you, and if they're not talking about you, then they're talking about your competitors.

How the lead generation cycle works to build your brand

Marketing elements do not operate in isolation from one another. Each social platform, blog, newsletter or video you produce does not stay on one singular platform but is shared across social channels and websites. An effective marketing system will take advantage of the crossover that occurs between your website, your social profiles, your email marketing, your traditional marketing and your customer service. In the corporate sphere, there's a tendency to compartmentalise roles and responsibilities. Traditionally, marketing and customer service have often come under different departments who then have to talk to each other when needed. However, this way of thinking is problematic when it comes to marketing your business in the social media age. I have developed a life-cycle diagram to show the cycle of how leads are generated when you use inbound marketing methods such as blogging to attract people to your business. You can see for yourself how marketing and customer service integrate.

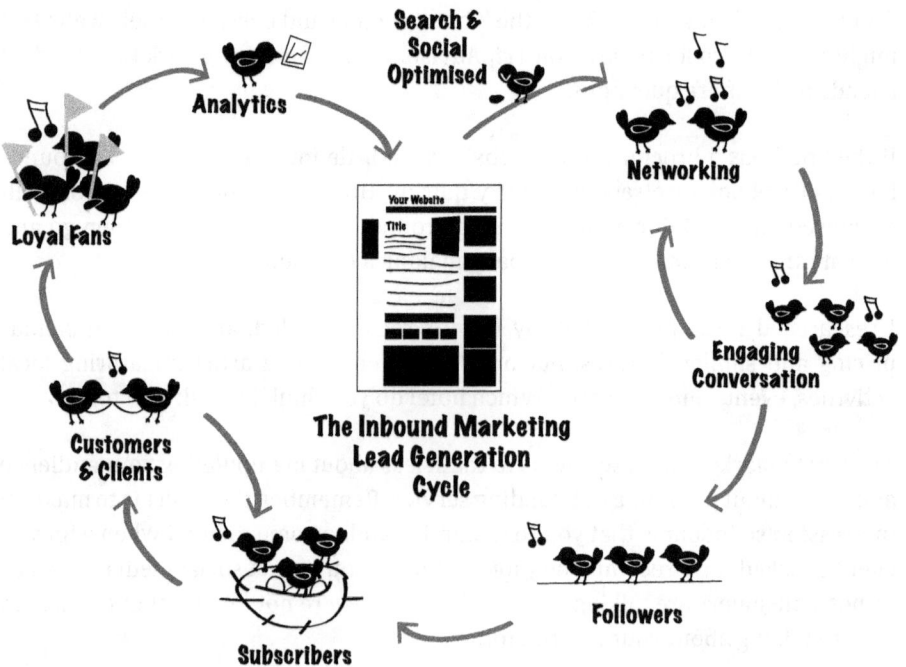

The Inbound Marketing Lead Generation Cycle

Search & Social Optimised · Analytics · Loyal Fans · Customers & Clients · Subscribers · Followers · Engaging Conversation · Networking · Your Website

Here's how it works when you share relevant, compelling content with your audience. Say you have established a blog on your website and you have created a blog post, made sure that it is search engine optimised, and have hit the publish button. What happens next? When you have an inbound marketing system in place, over time you will attract people with your powerful content. They talk about your content and share it with their friends and networks and attract more followers to your content. From that point, people are more likely to become subscribers so they can receive your content directly, and it is your subscribers who are most likely to buy from you. If your service is great, your happy clients will then promote your business for you through word of mouth on social platforms and by actively sharing your content. This then feeds more people into your marketing system and the cycle starts over for them.

The beauty of the lead generation cycle is that it doesn't rely solely on you doing all the work. As Michael Stelzner says in his ground-breaking book *Launch*, you are the spark and your happy clients are the fire. Yes, it takes effort to get going in the beginning, but by honing in on a clearly defined ideal client and generating content aimed squarely at that person, you will find you slowly need to do less to get the wheels turning productively.

The biggest problem I come across when I talk to other solo entrepreneurs using inbound marketing is that they aren't generating more sales, even though they are generating more activity. If your content marketing strategy is missing elements that help feed the lead generation cycle, you may not be achieving the success you could be enjoying if you had a cohesive and focused system in place.

Approaching your online marketing in a systematic way saves you time and generates more leads and sales. Your content can be the magnet that draws your ideal potential clients in, so you can nurture relationships with them. You may not realise that you even have content worth sharing. I can tell you right now that you do.

If your marketing is not going as well as you think it should be, consider formulating a new plan, one that is systematic, one that connects your marketing activities to each other and one that gets results. If you have yet to make the leap into business and are still getting things set up, you have a brilliant opportunity to get your marketing system in place before you build your business.

A healthy marketing system will help you get value from online channels without hassle and a heavy time investment. It will also enable you to grow your reach, your influence and your relationships with potential clients.

In order for this cycle to work effectively, there are five foundational inbound marketing strategies that need to be in place.

1. Create powerful content

You don't just want to create any old content for your business website, you are aiming for powerful content that hits the spot with genuine potential clients. You're also aiming for content that will be widely shared and that will take on a life of its own. Rather than produce content that perfectly represents your brand but stays static, aim for content that moves and even aim for content that can be altered through people's comments on social media, blog posts etc. Social media author Mark Schaefer introduced the concept about content that moves on his popular blog {grow}.

The most viral content on the internet has the following characteristics:

- It is human, real and raw
- It tells a story that people can relate to
- It isn't watered down to please factions or avoid controversy
- It is fuelled by your existing community

Creating 'content that moves', is relevant, powerful, and attracts more people to your business. This helps you grow your mailing list, inform and educate your prospects, and provide incredible value that builds your 'know, like, trust' factor.

Content creation comes in many forms and the strategies you choose will be informed by who your ideal client is. You could include branded content such as social media posts, graphics and infographics, promotional campaigns and competitions, product or program launches, irresistible subscriber offers, webinars, slideshows, emagazines, hard copy magazines, books, podcasts, teleseminars and more.

2. Curate valuable content

Curating valuable content helps to inform and educate your ideal clients so they can make an informed decision about investing in what you have to offer. Content marketing, one of the primary tenants of inbound marketing, is not all about *your* content. Building your likeability and authority also means being able to share quality content created by other people that you know will appeal to your prospective clients. In order to share quality content, again, you first have to have a thorough understanding of your ideal client, his/her favourite types of content, social hangouts etc. How do you find resources and information that really hit the spot with your ideal clients? Start by working out where your followers, subscribers and colleagues are hanging out online. Then observe who their heroes are and who they follow, then you follow these heroes and share their content. If you are starting from scratch and don't yet have a following on social media, sharing helpful content is a great way to gain momentum. If you can show that you share the most helpful, relevant content for your prospects, you will quickly become the go-to person in your niche.

3. Relate to your community

There is no point creating or curating content that is irrelevant to your prospects, followers and fans. It's essential to learn how to relate to your potential clients through social media and permission-based marketing, so you can develop rapport, get to know each other and get feedback on the burning issues that are important to them. These are the issues keeping your potential clients awake at night, issues you can help them with.

4. Repurpose your content in other formats

Once you've created and shared wonderful content that relates to your potential clients, it's important to leverage that hard work rather than reinvent the wheel. Every piece of content you produce or share should be used and reused again and again. If you have blog articles, turn them into an ebook. If you have an ebook that is getting good traction, turn the topic into a webinar. If you ran a terrific webinar that had lots of signups, have it transcribed and turn it into an ecourse. Create a video series from popular topics on your blog. Use your images on Instagram to populate your other social platforms. Turn your more popular podcasts into a product. Take quotes out of a book you write and turn them into memes for Pinterest and your blog. The possibilities are only limited by your imagination. The goal is to get maximum mileage out of every ounce of content you produce. So start thinking of ways you can repurpose your content. Rinse and repeat is the name of the game.

5. Review your performance

It's important to regularly review your performance on your website, email marketing system, Customer Relationship Management (CRM) system and social channels so you can evaluate how well you're meeting your potential clients' needs. The data provided through Google Analytics, Facebook Insights and other analytics tools can give you a lot of information about who you're reaching, how you're reaching them and what they are looking for.

Un-Career Story

Debbie's story below illustrates the importance of engaging with your community and the benefits to having a strong niche.

Debbie's Story

I found it difficult to balance a career at a senior level in financial services and being a mum. When I had a baby there was no way I was prepared to take a back-step in my career, and I attempted to go back to a challenging role four days a week. I hadn't factored in sleep deprivation or mother-guilt into this plan.

With the benefit of hindsight I probably should have outsourced more or asked for more help. However, when a redundancy became an option I jumped at it because spending the next two to three years negotiating new hours every year based on my child's changing schedule, or having to ask someone's permission to go to first days of school, kinder duty or look after a sick child just made me feel bored and tired.

I had been watching other women who had made the leap from corporate to small business with interest and figured it was now or never. When I looked around at opportunities, there wasn't something that already existed that grabbed me, so it was quite empowering dreaming something up and building a brand.

The business I started, Story Mama, is an online bookstore specialising in picture books for little kids. We just stock the best of the best, and all our titles have been read and reviewed. We have done all the research for a shopper, and found the award winners and the books you can be using as tools when your child is approaching a milestone like toilet training, getting a sibling or moving to a big bed. We offer quick delivery and make selecting the perfect book really easy.

Not having had a background in marketing, it took me a little while to find my feet in this area and find what worked. It has been a bit of a process of trial and error. We have used print advertising, social media, price comparison sites, email, search engine optimisation, Google Adwords, guest blogging, online advertising, giveaways and postcards. The most effective tool, although also expensive, has been Google Adwords, followed by advertising online in some well known gift guides. I like how trackable these options are which really lets you understand your return on investment. Social media, particularly Facebook, as well as email newsletters, have also really worked for us. They have been great at building an engaged community and building trust with our readership. Guest blogging has also been really useful as it drives traffic to the site without generally costing anything.

Currently, my biggest challenge is being a jack of all trades, from managing inventory, editorial, marketing, technology and strategy. Still, the autonomy that comes with all that is also good. It can just take a bit longer to figure things out when there isn't a help desk to ask. The best bit of small business is the lack of investment committees, meetings, and hierarchies. Being nimble is fun.

What keeps me going is reminding myself why I got started - being able to juggle my tasks and priorities as much as I like. Looking back at how far I have come and what I have learned so far in my small business adventures is also pretty cool. I love discovering new picture books and introducing a new generation to old favourites. I also love the customer interaction, be it in person, via email or social media.

Juggling my business with my family requires both discipline and planning. I have very structured work days with a list of bare minimum tasks that must be completed. If they are not done during the time allocated they have to be done at night. I make use of child care for my son as there is just no way I could achieve anything with him in the house, and I didn't think watching me work was much fun for him. I try and keep time with my little boy work free and make sure I disconnect, particularly from social media which is way too easy to stay connected to. I put the phone on "do not disturb" and turn the computer off to stop me straying.

If you're going to go down the business owner path, be realistic with your expectations. You are probably not going to replace a high salary instantaneously by going out on your own. There are other measures of success. Also, you may need capital not just to set up but to manage operating expenses in your first year. The best bit of advice I got when I launched and was all worried about failure, was 'you just don't let it fail'. That's been gold - if something isn't working, you need to tweak it, change it.

Debbie Hatswell from Story Mama storymama.com.au
lives in Melbourne, Victoria, Australia.

Ten marketing elements that feed the lead generation cycle

Let's break this marketing system down even further by looking at specific elements that work together to feed the lead generation cycle.

There are a number of tangible steps you can take to ensure your marketing efforts are connected and are working towards building your profile, increasing your visibility and growing your profits. Here are ten of the best:

1. Your own self-hosted WordPress website

Your website is like the aorta of your business. Your business activity revolves around it, and the fruits of that activity pour back into it, giving it life. If you don't have your own website, you may be compromising the health of your marketing system, not to mention your business.

Why have your own website?
Regardless of whether you create YouTube videos, podcasts or written blog posts, your website should be your business hub. Google loves fresh, quality content and your website is the place to store that content so your business can be easily found by prospective clients. Your website is your real estate. It's your space to

do with as you please. You can only ever borrow space on social networks, but when you regularly generate fresh content on your website, you are also giving your followers a reason to visit your website again and again.

Why a WordPress self-hosted website?

When it comes to business websites there are lots of options, but sometimes lots of options can result in confusion, and that means you end up doing nothing. I know, because if it weren't for the techy people in my life, I would have been at a loss when I first started out. Fortunately for you, I can share my experience, so you don't have to learn the hard way.

Trying to decide which platform is best can turn your hair grey, but once you figure out what you need, the choice becomes pretty clear. Ultimately, having a website and blog that you can fully integrate with your social media marketing, that performs well on search engines and that has the ability to brand, customise and monetise your efforts and is freely available to use, ie. open-source, is what you want. A self-hosted WordPress website is a great way to go and here's why:

You control the publishing platform

A self-hosted website is one that is hosted on a webhost that you pay a yearly fee for rather than on a third party hosting service. Rather than your site sitting on someone else's server that they control, it is sitting on a server that you control. For example, on Wordpress.com websites, Wordpress controls how much space you use and what you can do with the website. On a Wordpress.org website (which is the self-hosted version), you choose what server to host your website with, according to your needs for space etc. You control the domain and email addresses associated with that domain and you have complete control over the website content.

You can create a home for your content

A self-hosted WordPress website enables you to easily self-publish and share your own content to answer your potential clients' questions. Self-published content comes in all shapes and forms, from podcasts to written blogs. This varied content needs a home and that home is your website. Regularly updated content can be housed on your blog and one-off content can be made available through landing pages, which are stand-alone pages on your website.

> Blogging is about getting real and being real with your readers so they can learn as much as they can from you.

A note about business blogging: Some notable experts in content marketing would say that you shouldn't think of yourself as a blogger if you're writing content for a business audience. Business blogging is different to personal blogging. As a personal blogger, the focus is on what personally matters to you the most, your life and adventures, your challenges and triumphs, but as a business blogger your primary goal is to answer potential clients' questions and be a thought leader, or go-to person in your industry niche.

As a business blogger, you are writing and producing content for completely different reasons. Even if you have the best intentions and really want to help others, your content can still be viewed as self-promotional by a website visitor, purely because the information is housed on your business website. So it's a good idea to view your content as if you were a publisher producing a magazine or newspaper, rather than as a business. That doesn't mean you need to become the media, it just means you need to shift focus a little so that you are providing quality impartial content to help buyers make informed decisions.

Business blogging is not about delivering a one-sided view or looking at things from a rosy perspective. Blogging is about getting real and being real with your readers so they can learn as much as they can from you.

You can easily customise the look and feel of your site

The sheer volume of themes and plugins that you can customise will leave you feeling like you've just walked into a clothing store where everything fits and looks fabulous!

A theme sets the style and layout of your website or blog. It's the background colour scheme and dictates where your content sits on the page. When you're looking for a theme, you'll want one that is easy to update and customisable. WordPress.org enables you to use a ton of different commercial themes and theme frameworks that enhance your website's functionality and appearance. You can access done-for-you theme templates made by professional WordPress website developers. Theme options on Blogger, Typepad, Weebly and smaller platforms just don't compare when it comes to design and customisability.

You can easily integrate your site with social media

Social plugins make it easier for your content to be shared across the social web. Social media integration on your website means that you can utilise every inch of your website to build your following on social media. This in turn helps you build relationships with your potential clients and customers. WordPress offers incredible flexibility when it comes to social media integration.

Your can easily optimise for conversions

You can place 'call to action' boxes and pages in every nook and cranny. WordPress enables you to place 'call to action' boxes and ads in a variety of places on your website. thanks to custom widget areas. You can also easily create custom landing pages that are dedicated website pages promoting a single product or service. There are several brilliant plugins that enable you to create these with ease. An example of a landing page would be a page where you are asking people to opt-in for a free ebook or register for an event. This means you entice visitors to sign up for your mailing list or visit a landing page with incredible ease.

It makes SEO a piece of cake

There are a few brilliant SEO plugins that are available for WordPress. SEO is generally built into Wordpress.org theme frameworks such as the Genesis Theme Framework by Studiopress. If you use a theme framework and child theme, which is a theme that sits on top of the theme framework, it means you don't have to update it as regularly, all you need to do is type in the SEO tags, descriptions and titles with every post or page. You can also use plugins like Scribe from StudioPress or moz.com to help you find the right keywords and backlinks for your content. Another terrific aspect is that Wordpress.org blog posts are indexed quickly by Google. This is not the case with websites that sit on third party servers.

You can extend your site's functionality

You can easily extend the functionality of your website and turn it into a membership site. One of the key benefits of a self-hosted site is that you have the capability to turn it into a membership site. This enables you to monetise your website, so that you can earn passive income from products and programs and give members instant access to premium content.

You can integrate ecommerce into your WordPress site

There are now an abundance of options for integrating an online shopping cart into a WordPress website. This allows you to house your blog and also sell your products and services on the same website. Plugins such as Woo Commerce are free and easy to integrate.

2. Branding and design that compels your ideal clients to visit and revisit your website to learn more about you and what you offer

Branding and design will help attract the right people to your business and make it easy for them to find the answers to their questions. If you don't have branding that is squarely aimed at your ideal clients, you will end up attracting people who will never buy from you, or who do not value what you have to offer. A poorly structured website can confuse potential clients and blurry product images don't showcase your work. The goal is to be instantly recognisable across all of your social platforms and online media, and to turn that recognition into action.

3. Genuine potential clients following you on social media

People need a reason to follow you. What value can you provide that others can't or don't? Are you being responsive, answering questions, holding fun competitions or promotions? Can you solve your followers' problems with your content?

Once they are interested, it's vital to make it easy for people to follow you. Recently I came across a blog I really wanted to subscribe to. The thing is, there was not a subscribe box to be found, not even an RSS subscribe button. When I clicked on the blog's Twitter button, it went nowhere. I became frustrated and clicked away. If you have a blog, enabling people to follow you on social media and subscribe to your updates is a must. To do that, it helps to make it really obvious where you are hanging out online.

You don't necessarily have to place every social media button on your website, just those you have an active presence on. You can set up your system to automatically feed posts or images from one social platform to another using tools like ifttt.com or zapier.com

> You can't rush a real relationship without putting it in jeopardy.

4. A subscriber base so you can communicate with potential clients directly and build relationships

If you've been in online marketing for a while, you may have heard the expression 'the money is in the list'. But the thing is, even if you have a mailing list, you still need to build a relationship.

Lots of businesses, particularly online retailers, want fast results from their online marketing, but when it comes to building relationships, fast results are not the name of the game. If you make a sales offer to your subscribers too early, before you've had a chance to build a relationship with them, you may not experience the results you hoped for. You can't rush a real relationship without putting it in jeopardy.

How do you get started at building solid relationships that will lead to business?

Start by building your list

If you put time and effort into building your mailing list, the initial reward will be a dedicated group of potential clients you can talk to directly. To encourage subscriptions, offer something valuable to potential subscribers, something that will help them solve their problems. Many businesses offer ebooks or webinars or run competitions. Simpler ideas are cheat sheets or templates, coupons and vouchers, or even colouring-in pages for kids.

It really depends on what your business is and what your potential customers would value most. To find out, ask questions on your blog and on social media. Observe the issues and concerns that come up for your ideal potential clients.

Nurture your list

Having people sign up to your list is one thing, but nurturing the relationship requires you to reach out with helpful, valuable content on a regular basis. Use your emails to seek feedback, connect your subscribers to your social media activity, and share relevant, helpful content they can relate to. Share stories, and don't be afraid to share a little about yourself.

I used to find email marketing scary, mostly because it had the word 'marketing' in it. But what I've found is that it's a great way for me to share with others who are interested in my business and what I can offer them. As it becomes harder and harder to reach your audience on Facebook, due to declining organic reach, having an email list means you can communicate with your followers in a meaningful way, without it being a waste of your time or theirs.

You won't always get it right, but when you look back at your campaigns you'll start to see which emails are more popular, and can adjust your writing style and content accordingly.

If you don't yet have a mailing list, you can set up a simple one for free through MailChimp. If you want something more complex, MailChimp has a Pro option but there are also platforms such as Aweber and Constant Contact that may also meet your needs. Infusionsoft and Ontraport offer more complex solutions for small businesses that are really serious about using email to prompt growth.

5. Loyal fans and happy customers who can't help but like, share and shout out about what you do and say

A healthy content marketing system encourages fans and customers to share your information and insights with their networks. If you have nailed your customer service and offer incredible value, you will naturally attract a network of loyal fans who want nothing more than to help you succeed and shine. This is why customer service is an integral part of the marketing matrix. These days, people jump straight onto Twitter or Facebook to let everyone know a business has given excellent service, or has let them down. Third party review sites can also make the difference between whether someone buys from you or from a competitor.

6. A social media presence that is fully integrated with your website and offline marketing

When it comes to building your following, make sure your website's viewers, visitors and networks know you are on social media. Integrating your social platforms helps you attract genuine potential clients to your business and helps your brand stand out from the crowd. If you're everywhere, how can anyone miss you?

If you want to attract genuine fans to your social platforms, having a website which enables that to happen is a must! Having social media integration on your website also makes it easier for people to interact, comment and purchase from you.

But just how do you integrate your social platforms with your website? Well, fortunately there are a few fantastic tools to help you do that.

The Facebook like box

A like box is a widget that shows who likes your Facebook Page and includes a like button to encourage website visitors to like your Facebook Page. This means your potential clients don't need to leave your website in order to engage with you on Facebook. This is a huge plus and can drive a lot more qualified leads to your page.

As you know, people tend to like things their friends like, so, if someone sees their friends like your page, they are more likely to like it too. If you have a Facebook like box on your website, the faces that will show up in your Facebook like box will be that person's Facebook friends.

The fans who like your page via your website are more likely to be qualified potential clients and not just people liking you for the sake of it. If you are struggling with attracting genuine potential clients to your Facebook pages, and end up with likers who don't turn into leads, this strategy could make all the difference.

Social sharing buttons

Social sharing buttons on every blog post and page of your website enable your readers and followers to share your content quickly and easily. If you don't have prominent social sharing buttons, you are missing out on increased traffic to your website, guaranteed.

Facebook and Google registration and login

Many people don't log out of Facebook or Google, so if you have an online shop, consider enabling your customers to login to your site via either of these platforms.

Facebook email subscribe

If your email subscribers use their Facebook login email to subscribe to your email list, it enables you to target campaigns directly to them on Facebook. The email marketing platform Aweber.com enables Facebook email sign ups, so if a user is logged into Facebook, their mailing list signup form will auto-populate with their Facebook data.

Commenting systems for blogs

Commenting systems such as Disqus enable your readers to comment on your blog using their Facebook or Twitter profile. Their Facebook or Twitter profile picture will show next to their comment.

If you are commenting on someone else's blog for business reasons, this can add extra exposure for you. Ensure your business page is linked to your personal profile on Facebook, and then your business page link will show along with your comment.

You do not have to enable comments on your blog, and some brands are choosing not to, but if you want conversation on your website, it's a great way to encourage people to come back to it time and again.

7. Google Analytics and other data measurement tools

There is not much point to marketing anything unless you evaluate your performance. Using free tools such as Google Analytics and Facebook Insights can tell you a lot about the people you are attracting to your website and how well you are doing in terms of conversion rates. If your marketing is not hitting the mark, you can go back and tweak things. Marketing your business is a process of constant evaluation, tweaking and re-evaluating, and if something really isn't working, you can change course and start over.

8. Naturally search engine optimised blog posts and website

There is no great mystery to how SEO works, despite what some SEO marketers might lead you to believe. Search engines are quite literal and it's your job to tell them what your content is about. You have already narrowed down your ideal client and brainstormed their questions. Type those questions into Google and see which phrases come up the most and how many websites are competing with each other for the same keywords. For a fee you can use tools like wordtracker.com. If competition is high and the websites you're competing with are well-established, you'd be wise to vary your keywords and make them more specific. A way to make your keywords richer and more specific is to use long-tail keywords. These are phrases that involve three to five keywords, and sometimes more.

For instance, if you typed 'baby clothes' into Google, the results could be from anywhere. If you typed 'rock'n'roll' themed baby clothes Brisbane', the results would be more specific to the niche and location. The rankings change constantly, so make sure you check back in regularly.

To maximise your SEO:

- Use your long-tail keywords frequently and often
- Create relevant, quality, fresh content often via a blog
- Make sure your headings contain relevant keywords that spell out what the article is about
- Create backlinks to other content on your website and relevant content elsewhere
- Make sure your blog posts have a sprinkling of your keywords that are natural and relevant to your website

9. Media coverage through publicity

The media industry has undergone enormous change in recent years, but it still pays to gain media coverage for your business. It's usually free, and builds your authority and credibility.

Contributing articles

Consider writing articles for print magazines or newsletters that are focused on your area of expertise. For instance, if you design handmade products, you could write for one of the publications that focus on design, handmade arts and crafts, like Frankie Magazine. If your expertise lies in graphic design, there are literally hundreds of graphic design magazines and other trade publications. Trade magazines and organisational newsletters are often crying out for content. All you need to do is ask if an organisation would be interested in your contribution.

Media releases

If you have something newsworthy to share, it is a good idea to write a news release with prepared quotes included. Always start with the most important piece of information and leave the least important to the bottom of the release. It is a good idea to phone news outlets when you have news to share and ask who you should send a media release to, and how they prefer to receive it—there are still some journalists who prefer faxed releases. If you email an impersonal media release it is unlikely to be picked up by a journalist. Journalists receive hundreds of media releases a day and are much more likely to read and respond to a release that is addressed to them personally, and from someone they are familiar with.

Journalists love good media sources, so if you have a reputation for providing them with good story leads, interviewees and photo opportunities, you are more likely to be featured.

Sourcing media opportunities

There are two sites I recommend you check out when it comes to sourcing media opportunities.

1. Help a Reporter Out (helpareporter.com) which is US-based.

2. SourceBottle (sourcebottle.com.au) is an Australian-based PR opportunity website. Their daily newsletter provides a list of requests by journalists and event organisers for interviewees and also for goods for event goodie bags. This list is used by legitimate journalists so it is worth keeping an eye on.

10. Networking

It's so easy to get discouraged when your business's success or failure comes down to you and only you. That's why I'm thankful for the on and offline communities I'm a part of, communities that offer friendship, shared resources, wisdom and, importantly, business referrals.

Working for yourself can be a lonely experience, so it really helps to attend local networking events and industry conferences so you can meet other business owners, make friends, connect with potential clients and build industry connections. Meeting with people face-to-face solidifies relationships you may have started in an online community and gives people a chance to get to know you.

The prospect of dressing up and walking out the door to attend networking events may be a tad daunting for some. If you're an extrovert, attending networking events will probably come easy to you and leave you feeling energised. If you're an introvert, you'll have a great time, but you'll probably feel drained afterwards.

Because I struggle with interpersonal communication, I find attending networking events stressful. My anxiety levels go through the roof, and it takes all my energy to keep that from showing when I'm out meeting people. I do it anyway, though, because I understand the importance of connecting with people in real life, and I often walk away feeling like I've made new friends and deeper connections. It really is worth the effort, so even if you are an introvert, I encourage you to move outside of your comfort zone and get to networking events.

So, how do you make networking work for your startup business?

Identify exactly who it is you're trying to reach

Are you focusing on networking with potential clients, other people in your industry or joint venture partners? You'll probably find that each will attend different events or belong to different types of groups on and offline.

Commit to following up with people after attending an event

If you're going to collect business cards, make sure you follow up with people you connect with at a networking event. I use Infusionsoft campaigns to help me do this effectively. When someone gives me a business card, I scan it into Infusionsoft and add a tag that identifies the person as having attended a particular event. When I've finished adding people, I then run a campaign that invites them to join my mailing list. Once they've opted in to my mailing list, I then send them some further information and some free resources to help them learn more about what value I offer.

Check out value-added services to see if they meet your needs

Many on and offline networking communities and membership programs offer additional services, discounts, information and training that may be helpful for your small business.

Often groups appear to offer similar things, so look for the points of difference. Cheaper is not always better, but neither is really expensive. Check out the blogs and social media profiles of groups to get a better feel for how responsive they are. Sometimes small and local is the optimal way to go.

Watch out for fortune hunters and zealots

Some networking communities, both on and offline, are rife with fortune hunters and over-zealous network marketers. There's nothing wrong with wanting wealth or being passionate about your business, but if you get caught up in conversation with people who don't really care about connecting with you, other than to convince you to jump on board their cause or use their services, then your time may be better spent with other business owners.

Networking is a dance. You'll reap more rewards by patiently building relationships and showing genuine interest in others than handing out your cards to all and sundry, and trying to sell them on why your product or service is the best thing since sliced bread.

Un-Career Story

In her story, Chris shares about the power of relationship building through networking events.

Chris's Story

I had grown up in a dysfunctional family, so my childhood was a challenge to say the least. There are many stories I can tell about who was to blame and what went wrong, but the truth is I was given certain coping skills that I then took into my adult life. The primary coping skill was emotional manipulation, and by the time I reached my mid 20s it was becoming obvious that other people really didn't like me. I had some rude awakenings and some major emotional issues to climb over, and then started to see beyond myself and started to plan for my future. I sought professional help and made some headway. A few years later I felt strong enough to start a family. At 29 I brought a beautiful baby girl into the world. Of course, the natural expectation was that I would love motherhood and embrace this gorgeous child. That was not my experience. I didn't cope because I had not learned to have belief in myself. I hibernated for the first six months and then as soon as I could, I was back into full time work.

Over the next ten years I worked in various corporate level Administrative/ Quality Management positions, some full time and some part time. The most memorable day for me was a day in October 2008. It was a Friday morning and I was unceremoniously shown the door. It felt like it came out of nowhere, but on reflection I realised the stress of my workplace meant I had been defaulting back to my old emotional manipulative ways and creating major personality conflicts.

This is when my life took a completely new direction. The first thing I did was put more time and energy into myself and my own issues. I started to work on my emotions from an energetic perspective, although I didn't know what the outcomes were going to be. After a few months I really needed something to do, so I created a business to suit myself and my life; Balance Central was born.

Interestingly, I was soon offered a part-time position which allowed me to build my business while enjoying a certain level of income security. At the end of 2009 I was put in touch with a marketing coach. Between my energetic work and her ability to head me in the right direction, Balance Central started to gain momentum. That momentum came from one main area— networking. It was a good fit for my business as I needed to personally share the uniqueness of what I was offering. However, as an introvert I needed to continue working on myself and put some strategies in place so I could be a successful networker. After a few false starts, I soon discovered how easy it was to network effectively. Within a few months I was able to leave my part time job and focus solely on my business.

Networking, for me, is about establishing relationships and taking the time to genuinely care about others. I still have days when I need to push myself out my front door and sometimes it takes a good amount of planning and some strategising, but I love it, as the reward is in the relationships I build.

When I engage with someone, it's real, it's about them, it's about how I might be able to help. Often it is not about my own business but about referring them to someone else I know that can help. Sometimes it is simply being there to listen to the other person.

Networking is a little like shopping. When you walk past a row of shops, some days you walk into a shop and other days you just keep walking past. You probably love the shop and you probably love what they are selling, but you don't always want to go in. Networking is similar. People will like you but they won't always buy from you. People will come to you when they are ready. My favourite thing to do at a networking event is to show up. The more I just show up, the more people say, "I'm glad I saw you Chris, can you help me with ......?"

The key to becoming and continuing to be a successful networker is to be authentic. Be aligned with your strengths, be aware of who you are, and stay true to yourself. When you interact with others authentically, you automatically establish quality relationships. The quality relationships formed through networking have led to collaborations and joint ventures. This was only achieved through good, honest relationship building through networking.

Five years down the track I continue to network. It indirectly drives my success, so it's a vital part of my business plan. Networking allows me to share with others on a professional level, and allows me to keep growing. Whatever type of business you have, it is vital to understand the value you give through your business. A business, any business, is a vehicle for you to share your expertise. I am proud of my business and know that I am successful, not because of a dollar amount or how many clients I work with. I know I am successful because I wake up every day knowing I can continue to share my expertise in a consistent and professional way.

Chris Wildeboer is the owner of Balance Central
balancecentral.com.au, based in Brisbane, Queensland, Australia.

Bonus: Download bonus resources that dig deeper into this topic. For this chapter, I interviewed Adam Franklin, award winning entrepreneur, co-author of Web Marketing That Works and co-presenter of the Web Marketing That Works Podcast show. There's also a free Inbound Marketing Checklist and a printable affirmation to inspire you to take action now. To access these bonus resources, simply sign up here: bit.ly/uncareerresources

Chapter 8

Social media marketing fundamentals

Now that you know the elements to have in place for a healthy marketing system, we can dig a little deeper and focus on marketing your business effectively on social media.

There is little doubt that social media has changed the way businesses market themselves. However, a lot of people still baulk at using social media to market their business. The truth of it is that 73% of all internet users between 18 and 65 use social media, according to Pew Internet's 2013 research. Whether or not you have a social media presence, your potential clients are using it to find the information they need in order to decide whether or not to buy from you or your competitors.

Social media platforms are changing all the time, so these are general principals and strategies that can help you connect with people regardless of the social media channels you use.

Understanding how social media works

Instead of social selling, think social helping.

Instead of social selling, think social helping. Many small businesses jump onto social media wondering how best to sell their products and services. However, because the key to doing social media well is building relationships, being responsive and connecting with influencers, you'll have more success if you focus less on selling and more on helping.

Common social media faux pas

Below are the five most common mistakes that people make when using social media to market their business:

1. They self-promote at any given opportunity

Modern consumers have very little tolerance for flagrant self-promotion and yet, many business owners can't resist this when networking on social media. For example, when you jump on someone's Facebook page and say "Hi, look at me, look at me, visit my page," it's just like walking into someone else's shop and saying, "Well, this place sucks, come over to my shop!"

The truth is that self-promotion on other people's social profiles, in online networking groups and on blogs is a massive turn off. It shows people that you are only interested in yourself and don't care about them.

2. They fill their own page, profile or newsfeed with sales announcements

Social media channels can be terrific tools for building relationships with potential clients and strengthening relationships with current clients. However, a lot of businesses make the mistake of using their social pages as broadcasting platforms, constantly shouting out their services and products. Shift the focus to providing helpful resources, fun interactive games and storytelling, rather than boring followers to tears with sales content. You can definitely promote your business on your social channels, but if that's all you have to offer, people will quickly find something more interesting to engage with.

3. They focus on building their likes, followers or connections

The question that every business owner should be asking is, "How do I attract *the right people* to my social media channels?"

Every day, people ask me how to get more likes on Facebook, more followers on Twitter or more connections on LinkedIn.

To be brutally honest, these are the wrong questions. The right question, the question that every business owner should be asking is, "How do I attract *the right people* to my social media channels?"

The reason this question is more important is because the right people are more likely to become your clients. Trying to attract everyone will result in less engagement and fewer paying clients. If you want to drive more fans, more leads and more clients to your business, stop focusing on the number of people following you on social media and start focusing on the quality of people following you instead.

Why harvesting or buying likes or followers is a bad idea

It's true that the follower numbers on social media provide a measure of social proof, but focusing on the numbers can also be detrimental to your success on social media. When you first set up a social media channel it is tempting to harvest likers for your page by posting on lots of other pages, by participating in tagging games or worse still, buying likes and followers.

The number of likers and followers you have means nothing to your bottom line if those people aren't ever going to buy from you. In fact, focusing on the number of likers and followers you have can actually be detrimental in that you spend a lot of time and energy harvesting followers on other peoples' pages and profiles rather than focusing your attention on the people who already follow you.

Building relationships on social media is easy once you get started, but it won't result in overnight success. Social media marketing is a long-term strategy and one of at least ten elements that work together to ensure your marketing gets results.

4. They don't link promotions to a mailing list

Promotions and competitions can be fun, social and build buzz around your social media channel page or profile, and there is definitely a place for activities like these which are easy for people to participate in. However, if you're not feeding your followers into your mailing list, then you are missing out on nurturing deeper relationships.

Try running a variety of interactive competitions and sweepstakes on social media. On Pinterest, run 'Pin it to win it' campaigns, or announce competitions on Twitter a few times a day. Different platforms have different rules for promotions and they are constantly changing, so it's important to stay up to date.

On Facebook, if growing your list is your goal, it's more effective to run competitions on third party applications such as grosocial.com, woobox.com or fanpagecompetitions.com. These are customisable pages that are housed on the page tabs of your business page. You can also run competitions on your website or blog and alert people to them in your newsfeed through newsfeed ads.

Wherever you are running promotions, be sure to include information on how people can join your mailing list, so you can nurture the relationship.

5. They run frequent promotions and sales

Many businesses make the mistake of hosting a sale or promotion every other day or week. This kind of over-promotion can devalue your brand, and give the perception that you are cheap. Your fans will tire of '10% off' if it is happening all the time. Make your promotions special, seasonal events, and go big rather than frequent. A sale for 50% off that happens once a year is way more likely to attract potential clients than a sale of 10% off run once a month.

Customers tend to buy based on perceived value and not on price. Try writing sales copy in such a way that spells out what's in it for the customer instead of how cheap it is.

Simple, proven strategies for marketing your business on social media

I've talked about what most people do and why you would be wise to do things differently. Now it's time to share some strategies that really work, regardless of the social channel you use. These eight strategies work because they are based on sound relationship-building and storytelling principles. Many of these ideas work equally well face-to-face or in print.

1. Invest in social media ads

While traditional ads focus on reaching a broad audience, Facebook and LinkedIn ads allow you to do the exact opposite. Both Facebook and LinkedIn provide you with an opportunity to narrowcast in order to maximise conversions. Narrowcasting enables you to budget well because you focus on a highly specific niche market with every single ad.

If you use the Google Chrome Browser, you can also access the Power Editor tool on Facebook. This tool enables you to import your mailing list contacts into Facebook so you can target them directly. It also enables you to create highly targeted posts on your Facebook page. If you are yet to dive into Power Editor, I highly recommend familiarising yourself with this brilliant tool.

Social media channels are constantly updating how ads work on their platforms. If you want to stay up-to-date on Facebook Ads, jonloomer.com is a great blog to check out. For LinkedIn, I recommend you check out Viveka Von Rosen's linkedintobusiness.com website. While other social media platforms haven't quite caught up at the time of writing this book, it is worth keeping tabs on them also.

2. Use story arcs or sneak peaks

Using a strategic method to tell your story enables you to capture readers' attention and keep them hooked into what happens next.

What is a story arc?

A story arc is commonly used in fiction. Have you ever noticed that your favourite TV series often features mini-plots within a larger story? In a typical story arc, a great wrong occurs and the hero first tries to avoid fixing it because she doubts herself, then gets some gumption and tries to fix it, then fails and everything goes wrong, so she comes close to giving up. Then she is talked into trying again by a sidekick and she either beats the odds and saves the day, or a great tragedy ensues.

It's easy to form a story arc around a TV show, but with a bit of creativity, you can also create story arcs around your business. People relate to people and they love behind the scenes information and drama. For example, if you were getting ready to attend an event and your three year old vomited all over your dress, that makes for a funny story to share on social media. Your story arc might be:

Post 1: Eeek! I was all set to go out to Event X when my three year old gave me a hug goodbye and then promptly vomited all over my dress. I was supposed to be gone five minutes ago!

Post 2: 20 minutes later: I have nothing to wear!!!! Time to pull a rabbit out of a hat! And now I'm worried about leaving my three year old. What if he vomits again and I'm not here?

Post 3: 20 minutes later: All sorted! New outfit on and we're off! Three year old is totally fine and unperturbed! Ah, the life of a mum entrepreneur!

Another example might be a sneak peak where you reveal you are working on something, but don't give away what it is right away. Instead you might reveal little hints over a matter of days or weeks.

3. Customise your social media channels

New visitors are the mostly likely to thoroughly check out all your social channels. To maximise the value for the new visitor, customise your page on each platform, using these ideas as a starting point:

- On Facebook you can use page tabs as landing pages for promotions and competitions, share in-depth info about your business, leading people to find out more on your website

- On LinkedIn you can customise your profile or company page with images, links, and recommendations

- On Twitter you can customise your background and image header as well as your profile image

- On Google+ you can customise your header image, about section and profile image for pages and profiles

- On Pinterest you can customise your profile image and URL

Customising your social platforms also means you can give your profiles brand consistency, using the same colour schemes and imagery throughout to enhance brand recognition. This makes your brand instantly recognisable regardless of which platforms you have a presence on.

4. Create and share visuals that tell your story

Nothing tells a story better than a strong, clear image. Telling a story with words can be effective in the right context, such as on a podcast show, but telling a story visually is more likely to capture attention quickly. Images are highly shareable and given that scaling your marketing is the goal with social media, that's something to aspire to. Your images will be highly shareable if they are self-explanatory, so look for images that don't need a long blurb to explain them. They'll also be highly shareable if they are beautiful. Visuals with lots of white space attract the eye. Beautiful and funny images are shared more often than cluttered, blurry images or long monologues. Keep the appeal broad, and the humour to something everyone in your niche can relate to.

Types of images that do well on social media:

Infographics

An infographic displays complex information or research outcomes in graphical form. The infographic has become extremely popular since visual social media sites like Pinterest have taken off.

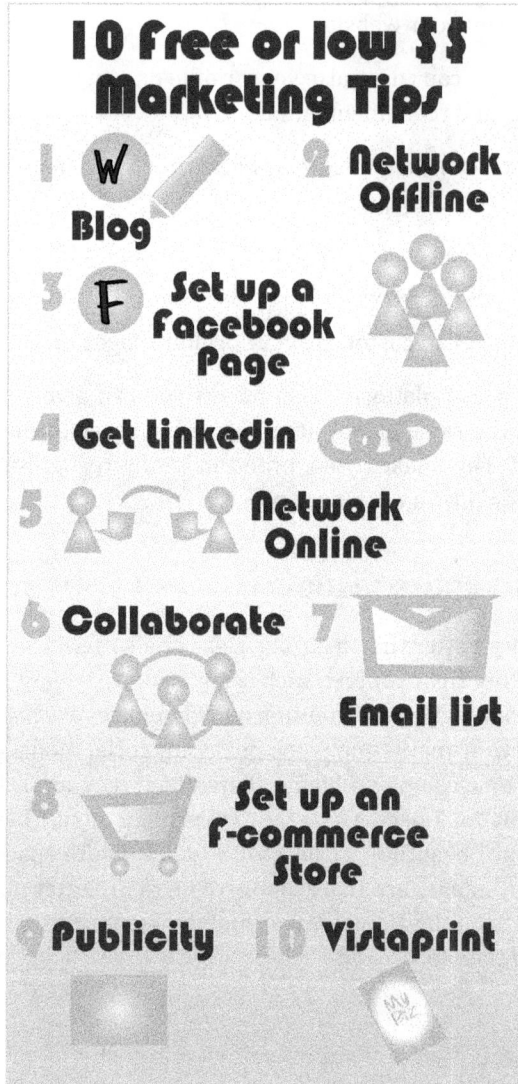

Behind the scenes photos

People love behind the scenes information about events, people and brands. Behind the scenes images add a human face to the work you do and as you know, people like to relate to people.

The Likeability Company
Posted by Caroline McCullough [?] · October 6

Phil and Cas are nerding out with software developer Bob Dunne from Youstak.com. #startup #fun #tech #takingovertheworld — at The Three Monkeys.

Inspirational, funny or helpful images that aren't stock images

Some of the most compelling and virally shared photos on social media have been simple visual statements about an event or an issue. You don't need to churn out lots of inspirational quotes to succeed at social media. Putting famous quotes on stock images has become popular in the past couple of years, but a more strategic approach would be to use your own images and be creative in how you present information, whether that be quotes or helpful information.

One of the most popular images I shared on social media was a cartoon graphic I created in about five minutes. I was up late at night and was musing on the fact that my work hours were totally out of sync with normal businesses. It seemed that the idea resonated with many others because the image was shared and re-shared more than 100 times. In fact, someone even removed my copyright and shared it as their own image—a big no-no, by the way.

WORK AT HOME MUM
HOURS OF OPERATION

4am to 7am

1pm to 2pm

9pm to 1am

*Please note, if you call at other times, you may experience poor call quality due to loud screaming in the background, and constant interruptions.

© 2012 supportawahp.com

Short videos

Our attention spans are short, so posting long-winded videos of you talking can result in less engagement than if you post a short video that gets straight to the point. Also, don't forget that you can also use presentations and demo videos in your social media marketing. If you have a Mac computer, you can use iMovie to create stunning videos without going to the expense of hiring a professional to do it for you.

Beautiful product images

Nothing sells a product better than a stunning image. Cluttered images, blurry photos and boring backgrounds will detract from the product you are advertising. Not every image needs to be on a white background; it really depends on the product. For instance, a fashion shoot in various settings can be really helpful for people trying to visualise how something will look on them. However, in many cases white space can really enhance products and make them stand out on social media. If you're selling products, choose the setting that is right for your products and your clients.

Travel-related images
People love to live vicariously through social media, so if your work takes you to stunning locations, cool restaurants and unique settings, use these images to increase interest in what you are doing. And, if you tag locations with hashtags, you'll often find that local tourism businesses and organisations will share and re-share your images.

5. Engage with other businesses on social media, but don't be salesy or spammish

Expand your reach and following by being seen on pages and in communities that relate to your business, but are not in direct competition with you. Engaging with other pages means to comment, like, respond, be helpful, add your two cents worth and show you care. Interact, converse, and ask questions, but don't sell your stuff unless you are specifically invited to, and even then, keep it to a minimum.

> Go for conversation over self-promotion and you'll spark people's curiosity, and naturally attract them to your pages and profiles.

People will naturally be drawn to you if you can solve their problems, and show empathy towards them. Other businesses won't mind you interacting on their pages in this way, as it is not about stealing attention away from them, rather it's about contributing out of a desire to help others.

Go for conversation over self-promotion and you'll spark people's curiosity, and naturally attract them to your pages and profiles, but demand they visit you, or promote your stuff on someone else's page or profile and it'll just turn people off.

Introducing yourself
Think about how you interact with a business when you first like their page.

A pushy and disengaging start would be to say, "Hi, Sarah Smith here from Blackbutt. Please return the favour and friend me on Facebook to help me look more popular".

You might say, "Jane Jones referred me to your page. Wow! I love those pink hats you make. They're gorgeous! Look forward to seeing more of your range in future".

If you are posting as your page, the same rules of etiquette apply. Think about whether you are making a genuine connection, or a sales pitch.

On my business pages, I seldom acknowledge and often delete introductory comments if they involve a spiel about how wonderful their business is. I always acknowledge and respond to an introduction which is focused on the reason why that person has liked or followed my page, or the things they love about my business. Let's face it, who wouldn't respond to a compliment?

Refer to other businesses by making it all about them and not about you

If you're posting about another business, do it from your own page so that your clients and likers can go and check it out for themselves. Take time to look at the services each business offers, focus on one thing and talk about that. It is much more meaningful, both to the business you are referring to and your likers.

Referrals have the greatest impact when they are individualised and relevant. For instance, you might like to thank the photographer who took your business shots on your Facebook page and tag her in the post.

On Twitter, if you participate in things like Follow Friday, forget tagging a bunch of businesses. Mention one or two and give some context to why you're tagging them. That will encourage others to follow them.

Here's a post that tags another business without spamming them:

Your Brilliant Un-Career shared a link.
Posted by Cas McCullough [?] · a few seconds ago

Love this! Women everywhere are becoming entrepreneurs and making a difference to families and communities... Great find on She Owns It.
https://www.facebook.com/sheownsit/posts/743418039041190

Female entrepreneurs 'an amazing engine for economic growth' | Mark Anderson and Sabine Cessou
www.theguardian.com

Economically empowering women benefits community as businesswomen reinvest profits in social goods, says head of international trade body. Mark Anderson and Sabine Cessou report

6. Avoid being boring

There's a difference between having consistent branding across your social platforms, and being boring. Change things up on a regular basis. On Facebook, change your cover image often—see it as a photo to be shared rather than a banner ad. Use it for sharing special offers and link to your mailing list or to a micro-site for a specific competition or offer.

Change your Twitter profile to reflect what you're up to at the moment and change your banner image frequently. When I run a new webinar, I usually promote it with a bit.ly link in my Twitter profile, as well as in the news stream.

Think of some fun things you can do to build relationships with your peers and followers. Don't take yourself too seriously, unless of course, your ideal clients do.

7. Participate in online networking groups that your ideal clients and peers participate in

In addition to attending face-to-face networking events, look around for special interest groups your ideal clients frequent. This could be on Facebook, Google+, Twitter, LinkedIn or a niche social networking platform like researchgate.org for researchers and houzz.com for people interested in home renovations.

Do your research: Work out where your customers and business associates hang out

If your ideal client hangs out on Twitter or LinkedIn, then be there. If the conversation around your industry is mainly on Facebook, then that's where you need to be.

Pick two social media platforms and stick to them

Rather than spreading yourself too thin, it pays to pick just two platforms where you can focus the majority of your attention. Work out which platforms your ideal clients use the most and focus on these.

For instance, if you are targeting professional women who are consultants, you might want to spend more time on LinkedIn and on high profile business blogs aimed at women.

If your target market is stay at home mums who use cloth nappies, check out cloth nappy forums as well as relevant groups on Facebook for mums into attachment parenting and the environment.

When you are networking with other business pages on Facebook, don't limit yourself to posting on other people's pages and building likes. You may well be missing valuable opportunities to build relationships with your ideal customers and clients: the ones who'll come back to you again and again, who'll rave about your business to their friends and networks.

When you do visit other social media pages, boards and profiles or share them with your fans or followers, ask yourself whether they relate to your ideal customer or client. If the answer is no, reconsider how you're networking on social platforms. If the answer is yes, then you'll keep your ideal clients engaged and wanting to come back for more.

Facebook groups

There are a number of networking pages and groups on Facebook. You just need to find the right ones for you. Do a search for a networking group that is relevant to your business or geographical area and ask to join. Each networking group has posting rules and guidelines. Make sure you familiarise yourself with these before diving in. If a group is not well moderated, move to one that is, so you don't waste your time wading through spam.

I belong to five main networking groups and these have translated into real-life networking and business opportunities.

Once you have joined, participate and get to know the other people in the group. The more you answer people's questions, the more insight you can gain on how they are thinking and what they are struggling with. You can then use creative ways to get conversation going on your business page based around the issues and questions you know your market cares about.

Twitter chats or tweetups

One of Twitter's big strengths is that it facilitates networking at live events, whether they are events run on Twitter or elsewhere. If you've missed something at a conference or on a webinar, just do a hashtag search and, bam! There's the stream of notes people have published on Twitter. You can then pick out one-liners and retweet to your followers. Retweeting during conferences is also a great way to connect with influencers. Everybody loves their business content to be retweeted. Joining special interest chat sessions on Twitter is also a terrific way to share ideas and connect with people in your niche. There are regular chat sessions on a number of different topics. You just need to find the right ones for you.

Google+ communities

Google+ communities foster in-depth conversation about different topics. People are drawn together over common interests rather than common people as they are on Facebook. There are several groups I've joined on Google+ where I didn't initially know anyone. I belong to a photography group, a poetry group and several marketing and entrepreneur groups. Google+ communities can be organised into categories, much like a forum, and posts in public communities are searchable on Google. Hot tip: Being active in these groups is good for SEO.

LinkedIn groups

LinkedIn groups are great places to build relationships with colleagues and potential joint venture partners. If you work in business to business, you'll definitely want to connect with others through relevant LinkedIn groups. The more you participate in groups on LinkedIn, the more opportunity you have to make new, meaningful connections. Take time to find the right groups for you. Some groups are more like job boards and spam havens, so be selective and go for the well-moderated groups.

Commit to interacting and responding to people within online groups regularly

If you're going to take the time to join a networking community, make sure you get the most out of it. When you commit to interacting on a regular basis it gives other business owners an opportunity to get to know you and what you have to offer without you having to sell to them. This is where the value lies: just like using social media, it's about engaging in meaningful conversation and building trust and rapport, rather than selling.

8. Ask simple questions that encourage debate

One day I posted a polarising question on one of my Facebook pages that ended up with 77 heated responses within two hours. What was the question? Which type of baby carrier people preferred.

If you are observing the issues that are important to your audience, you will be able to identify trigger points for debate. The idea is not to aim for controversy, but to talk about issues that matter to your audience.

Action Steps

Create three Facebook posts aimed at increasing engagement on your page

Create a funny/inspirational quote to share

Ask a polarising question: i.e. Polka dots or leopard print?

Create a story arc or sneak peek where you reveal a portion of a story, a step at a time

Find and join a social media community and start interacting

Bonus: Download bonus resources that dig deeper into this topic. For this chapter, I interviewed Donna Hamer, creator of the Fanpage Competitions App and author of two Amazon best selling books on social media marketing. She really shows how it can be done! There's also a free Social Media Marketing Checklist and a printable affirmation to inspire you to take action now. To access these bonus resources, simply sign up here: bit.ly/uncareerresources

Chapter 9

Keeping your customers coming back for more

Are you repelling business?

I needed to get some ideas together for a new client who wanted to rebrand his business, so I jumped onto fiverr.com.

I found a great designer who put together a couple of concepts for me, but when I asked her how much she would charge to do the vector images - logos or graphics that can be manipulated and resized without affecting the image quality - she replied that her package only included Photoshop files, and that was that.

Perhaps she lacked the software to do vector images – I don't know, but I was disappointed and couldn't help but wonder how much income she could be missing out on by not leveraging her initial discounted service to earn more money.

Are you repelling business by being too rigid in what you offer? If so, you may be missing out on business.

Repelling potential clients is not something anyone does intentionally, so pay attention when a client is communicating with you and see where you can go the extra mile to help them.

Here are a few questions to help you take a deeper look at how you're communicating with potential clients:

1. How rigid is your product or service?

If you have flexibility in the way you customise your service or products for potential clients, does your information make this clear?

I don't mean flexibility on price. Never let a customer talk you down on price. If that happens, they don't value you or your product and will always wait till you drop your prices. The flexibility that makes a difference is in how you tailor your products and services to your clients' needs. Make sure that if you can offer a bespoke solution, you let your clients know in your marketing materials.

2. Are you listening?

Are you reading your inquiry and customer service emails thoroughly? Are you picking up the phone to clarify grey areas with customers and potential clients? Are you reading and responding to their posts on social media?

The personal touch is important, and so is really honing in on your clients' issues or needs. If you're ambivalent, it will show. Customers can always tell when the person on the other end of the phone doesn't care about them.

3. If you met yourself as a businessperson at an event, would you want to talk to yourself?

Sometimes the problem is not that you're being too ambivalent, it's that you're being too pushy.

We've all met pushy people who just won't leave us alone. They can't help but pitch something at any given opportunity. Their conversation is about them and they aren't interested in you.

Pushy people look at every connection and every conversation as an opportunity to manipulate the discussion so that they can talk about their business, or worse, put prospects on the spot so that they have to say 'no' in public.

If you focus on helping and serving others, the right clients will love you and ask more about what you offer anyway. But if it's all about you, whether that be on social media or in person, they will soon want to walk away.

★ Action Steps

How flexibly are you able to be to meet your clients' needs?

Next time you talk to a potential client, take note of how well you actively listen to them. Are you reflecting back what they say to you? Are you writing down their key issues and concerns?

Creating a responsive culture

Social media's dominance in our lives means that customer feedback is instantaneous. If a client has a negative experience, they'll spread the news faster than you can boot up your iMac. Conversely, if a client has a positive experience, you want to make it easy for them to give their feedback so you can publicise it as a testimonial. It is therefore imperative that you establish processes to ensure you respond to requests, comments, glowing testimonials, questions, problems, setbacks and stuff-ups appropriately and in a timely manner. Make the most of every opportunity to respond to feedback.

What is a responsive culture?

Creating a responsive culture can enhance your reputation, profitability and, importantly, the longevity of your client relationships. A responsive culture means communicating with your stakeholders quickly and often, and ensuring you meet your customer's needs to the best of your ability. Your goal should be to make the service experience a straightforward, pleasant and enjoyable one for your customers, even when unforeseen events and service failures occur.

Why create a responsive culture?

Creating a responsive culture for your business from the outset will have a ripple effect on every person you come into contact with as your business grows and develops. It will also have an impact on your customers' experiences and perhaps make the difference between the customer offering repeat business or not. Many businesses fail to see each customer's spending potential in the long term. The fact is that your loyal customers and clients will spend thousands on your business if you consistently meet their needs.

Key qualities that will enable you to be responsive to your stakeholders are:

- reliability
- trustworthiness
- efficiency
- accountability

Reliability

Reliability means being able to deliver what you promise, on time, every time.

Reliable businesses promise what they can actually deliver, they keep their word, they respond to emails within 48 hours, they do whatever it takes to meet customer expectations. Be clear what your businesses' service framework is, so you can confidently stick to it. Ensure you are punctual, clear about your terms of service, and easy to get hold of by email or phone.

Trustworthiness

Trustworthy businesses have great testimonials publicly available on a website, in brochures and in other promotional materials. They enjoy fantastic word of mouth sales leads, as well as referrals from related businesses and happy customers. They value their reputation and will do whatever it takes to uphold it. Be sure to ask your customers for testimonials when they are overjoyed at the service you have offered.

Efficiency

Efficiency means streamlining your processes and making it easy for people to buy from you: the fewer steps the better. Make sure people can get hold of you in a variety of ways. Ensure your procedures are clear and consistent. Do your research on ecommerce options to pick the software that best meets your customers' needs.

Accountability

Accountability is ensuring that you stand by your words and actions and do your best to correct service errors. Offer a guarantee, or alternatively a really convincing argument as to why not. At the very least, ask for feedback on your service and offer discounts or bonuses to those who take the trouble to respond. Reward your loyal customers with VIP rates and communicate with all stakeholders openly and honestly.

★ Action Step

Take a few minutes to think about your customers' experience. Are you meeting their expectations or are you falling short? Which areas are you doing well in? What are the key problems people are experiencing? What are some steps you can take to improve customer experiences?

Planning for unforeseen events, catastrophes and service failures

As a consumer, I've learned that the best thing you can do when customer service goes wrong is to ask the question: "How do you plan to make it right?" As the owner of a business, it is helpful to view that question as a business planning tool. Service errors, catastrophes and a plethora of unforeseen circumstances do happen, and can hamper client service experiences, no matter how consumer-focused you are.

Planning for service recovery makes sense on many levels. Providing a quality service when things go wrong not only gives you a better chance of retaining the customer but creates an opportunity for them to recommend your business rather than complain about it to their friends.

Things to consider when writing a service recovery plan

Go against your own policies

One Christmas, an Etsy customer in the US messaged me to let me know that her parcel hadn't arrived after the promised ten days. I was heartbroken, because I loved the products she had purchased and really wanted her to enjoy them in time for Christmas. In the end, despite a written policy stating that I did not refund for items lost in the mail, I refunded the money she had paid. Luckily for the both of us, the items showed up just a few days later and the customer was really happy that I cared so much. She ended up repaying the refunded amount.

Communicate, communicate, communicate

If a problem you are trying to solve takes a bit longer to sort out than you envisaged, it is vital that you keep your customers updated regularly, and I mean every day. They want to know you're working on the problem. As soon as the problem is taken care of, get back to them straight away, if possible by phone.

Focus on solving the customer's problem, not on token giveaways

One year the kids and I were super excited to attend a winter festival in Brisbane. The three-day event featured an outdoor ice skating rink with snow flurries and a wonderland of international cuisine. What spoiled our experience was a major service let-down due to equipment failure. The event organisers' response was to give us free drink vouchers and promise that we'd be first in line when we returned the next day. The next day the same thing happened and I'd already spent a small fortune on bus fares, plus a few hours of my time, only to tell my disappointed children that we had to go home again. As this was a pretty special event that the kids were keen to attend, we tried a third time, and despite the fact that the kids were able to skate and thoroughly enjoyed the fake snow and hot chocolates, I couldn't help feeling disappointed with the organisers' response. A good service recovery response would have been to refund the money I'd spent or give my kids an additional free ice-skating session. That kind of response would have solved my problem of stress, loss of money, time and inconvenience. Giving us free drink vouchers felt like tokenism and not a true reflection of my value as a potential repeat customer, and all the customers they would get through my good recommendation. Needless to say, we never attended again.

Follow up with your customers

Following up after a service incident has been resolved is a great idea. Not only does it give the client an opportunity to give their feedback, which can help improve your business, but it allows them to feel heard, and to know that you care about them. A quick phone call or email to find out if the response to their problem was satisfactory and asking for feedback is often appreciated.

Recognise that mistakes are opportunities to improve your service

We want everybody to love us but sometimes that's just not going to happen. When you run your own business mistakes will be made, but it's important to look at them as opportunities to fine-tune aspects of your business that aren't working well. They are a reminder to clarify policies and better communicate with clients in the future. It is always good to let those affected know how you intend to improve your service. Customers appreciate it when you're humble enough to admit you are wrong and take their feedback on board.

Understand that sometimes there are difficult customers

I hate to say it but it is true. Balance your outstanding customer service with healthy self respect, and value what you have to offer. If you know you don't deserve the negative response from a customer, it is probably better to cut ties swiftly and walk away with your head held high. At times like this, having clear written policies and clear contracts are important so you know you've met your obligations.

Planning for service recovery is an excellent way of focusing your attention on meeting customer needs and expectations and on growing your business into what you want it to be.

Action Steps

- What strategies have you seen businesses apply that turned you from a disappointed customer into a satisfied and raving repeat customer?

- What strategies can you apply in your business to recover from possible service errors?

Bonus: Download bonus resources that dig deeper into this topic. For this chapter, I interviewed Josh Clifton, customer experience specialist, author of Mastering Front of House and blogger at masterhost.com.au. There's also a free Customer Experience worksheet and a printable affirmation to inspire you to take action now. To access these bonus resources, simply sign up here: bit.ly/uncareerresources

Chapter 10

How to accelerate your growth

There are a number of great strategies around to ramp up your conversion rates so you can attract qualified potential clients more quickly. The key is not to do every strategy you read about, but to choose those that suit your personality, lifestyle, abilities and business, then commit to following these through.

Email marketing

I used to be an email marketing scaredy-cat. The thought of emailing potential clients made my skin crawl, and I'd break out in a cold sweat at the thought of hitting the 'send' button. Eventually I decided to battle my email marketing demons and overcome my phobia, and the results have been phenomenal.

Not only do I now have active and engaged subscribers who email me back after I've emailed them, but sales have increased substantially.

Small businesses that struggle with email marketing typically make the following mistakes:

- They only email every few months, if at all

- They only email about sales, discounts and company news

- They don't use a reputable email marketing service that complies with current email laws and best practices

So, how can you tackle the email marketing monster? By taking action now, you can get seriously ahead of the game and improve your conversion and retention rates dramatically. Aside from using the right tools, there are three key strategies you need to know in order to blitz email marketing.

1. Attract more subscribers and increase your open rate by adding value

Provide valuable content that answers your potential clients' and customers' questions. Aiming to solve their problem and address their concerns makes people feel you are helping them and they will appreciate you, even if they don't buy from you right away.

You could exchange signup to a mailing list for a valuable piece of information in the form of an ebook, a checklist, an ecourse or a webinar. Members of your mailing list could be offered access to subscriber-only events. If you sell consumer goods, you could provide a subscriber discount on future purchases or give away samples.

2. Keep subscribers actively engaged by providing relevant content

In order to truly add value, you first need to understand what your subscribers want from you. You can figure this out by asking them regularly what they think. Use social media and your blog to ask your followers what their biggest issues are in the areas you work in. Then, when you email your mailing list, keep the content squarely focused on meeting your clients' information needs.

3. Prevent email overload by doing both 1 and 2

As email marketing has grown in popularity, subscribers have reduced the amount of emails they actually open. However, studies by Experian over the past few years show that marketers who put customer relationships first, who emailed industry news and 'how-to' content, and who emailed consistently, outperformed their counterparts by 50% or more.

So, don't be afraid to communicate with your subscribers regularly. If you are providing valuable, relevant content, they will love opening your emails.

By focusing on building longer-term relationships with your subscribers, rather than fly-by-night sales, you will improve your chances of increasing sales dramatically.

To pop up or not to pop up?

I have a love/hate relationship with pop-ups. Pop-ups are little windows that pop up when you are trying to read a blog post. They usually invite you to subscribe to the site's mailing list. As a reader, I hate pop-ups when they are intrusive, when they won't shut, when they pop up on my iPad just after I've started reading an article and when they are spammy and salesy. As a marketer I love them, when used appropriately, because I know that conversion rates are higher when you have one on your website.

If you don't want your readers to be annoyed at your pop-ups there are some things you can do to make them less annoying and perhaps even enjoyable. Make sure you customise the settings so they display after 30 seconds. You don't want to block someone from reading the blog post they were interested in. Offer something valuable and eye catching in the pop-up window to be clear that you are not about wasting people's time. There are plugins that put the pop-ups at the top or bottom of the window or that display off to the side if you prefer that option. If you decide pop-ups aren't for you, you can always do what I've done in the past and place your subscribe form in strategic locations around your website - up the top right hand side, in the footer and in an after post ad widget. Really, all you need to do is make it abundantly clear that you want people to subscribe to your mailing list. How you do that, at the end of the day, is up to you. Do what works for you!

Action Steps

Which of the three strategies could you implement to improve your email marketing right now?

Referral marketing

How to run a successful affiliate program

We've talked about joining others' affiliate programs, so now let's explore whether an affiliate marketing program is right for your business. This is a referral program where you pay a percentage of profits to others who actively promote your business, program or product. Your affiliates are previous clients or other businesses you have a relationship with and they refer you to other people in their networks.

Affiliate marketing has suffered some damage to its reputation through pyramid schemes or when it's used to manipulate a buyer to purchase who may not be a good fit for the product or service. However, affiliate marketing can be a perfectly legitimate way to promote your business.

Those who sign up to your affiliate program will help you reach a new audience that you would not otherwise have had access to. In effect, it is inexpensive advertising. Rather than paying for advertising in the hope that you'll get a return on investment, you only make a payment to your affiliate when you make a sale through their unique affiliate links.

There are plenty of online tools to help manage your affiliate program. Here are some tips to get you started:

- Approach businesses and individuals who you already have a relationship with and you know love your work

- Have guidelines in place for those who sign up as affiliates. Let them know what is okay and what isn't. Many affiliate programs have clauses to prevent unethical practices, such as affiliates buying a product or service through their own affiliate link

- Let people know about your affiliate opportunity on your website and point them to an affiliate link on your footer menu. Those who really want to promote you will go looking for the link

- Provide resources for your affiliates to use, such as email marketing templates, social media posts, and advertising images

- Email your affiliates to keep them informed about upcoming opportunities. One of the best programs I am a part of sends me my unique affiliate links and marketing copy in an email at the start of a campaign, and at key points throughout the campaign

- Provide your affiliates with incentives to promote your upcoming campaigns. Friendly competitions to pit affiliate against affiliate can be fun and motivating

- Pay your affiliates promptly after each campaign. If you schedule payments into your calendar for the end of each month, it will be easy to get payments out on time

Other referral methods

Some businesses lend themselves to affiliate marketing and some don't. In the latter case, you may want to set up agreements with specific businesses that are aligned with you.

Referral circles

Some businesses have referral circles where they only refer people to others within the circle. The circles are established by businesses that have common philosophies. This is common amongst health and wellbeing practices. You don't have to wait to be invited into a circle, although in some cases you may want to if the right circle is already set up and looking for new businesses to join them. You can set up your own once you've had time to get to know other business owners.

Reciprocal agreements

If you are unable to take on a client for whatever reason, or you feel that someone else would be a better fit for them (e.g. they aren't in your ideal client range), you could set up reciprocal agreements with a competitor. Some people might baulk at this idea but it is a terrific way to build relationships with your peers and work together so that everybody benefits.

Action Steps

Research options for running your own affiliate programs. Compare sites like ejunkie.com, sellfy.com and Premium Webcart (pwcart.com) to see what programs appeal to you.

Collaboration and joint ventures

When you collaborate, wonderful things happen and everybody wins.

Having been in business for myself for a while now, I have observed some interesting behaviour regarding collaboration and competition within the small business sector.

On the one hand, I've experienced and seen people be amazingly supportive of each other, lending a hand, an ear and even an arm and a leg to help other businesses. I've been blessed to be on the receiving end of wonderful, collaborative partnerships.

On the other hand, I've witnessed high school. Yes, high school all over again, folks. Gosh, I never wanted to revisit that again, but some sectors of small business seem to have it all–cliques, competition and lots of judgement and gossip.

As small businesses, we're all in this together. We should be doing all we can to help one another. When you collaborate, wonderful things happen and everybody wins. One person alone can only do so much, but when you work together, magic happens.

One of the key ways businesses can collaborate with each other is through events. Whether you run live events, training seminars, conferences or webinars, collaboration can enrich events by bringing talented people together. You can collaborate on events that support a charity or cause you feel passionate about, events to launch a new product, service or book, run joint seminars and workshops and more.

A fashion designer I know wanted to run a fashion parade in her town. A fashion parade is an event that takes a lot of collaboration to bring together. She worked hard to develop relationships with her competitors, other designers and marketers, so they could work together to bring the event to life. If lots of people didn't help out, this type of event would not get off the ground and everyone would miss out. The result was an incredible event that showcased everybody's designs and wares. Everyone enjoyed more business as a result. It was a win for the designer, a win for the other designers and a win for the town as the event attracted media attention and people from outside the town.

I've had the experience of being shot down when I've approached another business about a collaborative venture, and it's not fun, but, at the end of the day, every business needs to choose who they align themselves with and how. There is no point chasing people down who don't want to work with you. You're better off spending your energy on people who do.

If you assume everybody wants to stake their claim and ward off intruders, you'll miss out on building some incredible relationships. However, if you take the time to get to know others and look for the synergies, magic will happen.

So, don't be afraid to get out there, attend networking events and participate in networking activities on Facebook groups and in Google+ communities and the like so that you can meet other like-minded business owners.

If you bring your competitors into your fold, you will find that you each attract the right people for your respective businesses. Joint ventures are prime opportunities for everyone, because you each have your own email marketing databases you can plug people into.

Working with joint venture partners on events means that you can each combine your products or services to make amazing, value-packed offers that result in higher conversion rates and sales for everyone.

The old days of looking over your shoulder are gone. Collaboration is key. Do it and you will be well rewarded.

Ideas for collaborating with other businesses

Businesses can collaborate in many ways. I collaborated with a few business people in the Queensland Business Facebook group to come up with this list of ideas for you:

Service exchange

Businesses can collaborate through an agreed service exchange. While this can seem like an appealing prospect, be aware of the pitfalls. Often if something is free, it has a lower perceived value than if it was paid for. Service or energy exchanges work best when you have a particular need that the other person can meet and vice versa. Energy exchanges should not be entered into lightly and you should have a contract or letter of agreement so it is clear what each party expects from the other.

Mastermind groups

Mastermind groups are small groups of business owners who meet regularly to discuss issues they are having with their businesses. They can either be peer-led or led by a mentor. Mastermind groups can help keep you accountable to your goals, vision and objectives. They work on the basis of mutual support rather than top-down mentoring.

Content co-creation

Businesses can support each other by:

- guest blogging on each other's websites
- commenting on and sharing articles via social media

- accepting interview requests for podcast shows
- offering to interview someone to help them raise their profile
- working together on list-building activities such as webinars and tele-classes

The opportunities are only limited by your imagination.

Action Steps

Make a list of businesses you'd like to collaborate with. What qualities would you look for?

Un-Career Story

The following story illustrates the power of collaboration in accelerating business growth.

Christine's Story

Over many years working in employment services I became increasingly frustrated working within the confines of big business that focused on compliance rather than the clients' needs. My 'aha' moment came when head office decided to offer a hamper for increased productivity for the month of October.

They were looking for a 300% increase in work placements. I had always achieved my quarterly KPIs in the first six weeks of the quarter, and earned every bonus. What they didn't realise was I used to run a hamper business, so I was able to work out the real cost. The hamper was worth around $100, and compared to the usual bonus of $100-$200 per placement, was an insult.

I looked at what made me really successful at my job and started building a training business. Soon I handed in my notice, walking away from a well-paid secure position with only $20,000 worth of business arranged. I spent some quality time in the garden, put together a program and approached another employment services provider who I had worked for previously. They agreed to help me start up a work experience program in the hospitality industry that encompassed all the best elements of my skills and knowledge. I have now been operating for three years with automatic rollover contracts, have a chef that works with me and a part time admin person.

We love what we do and are really proud when one of our jobseekers obtains work or even feels empowered to make a life changing decision. Our slogan is "Transforming lives through food". We now provide free, fresh food parcels and weekly community meals to local disadvantaged people, and will soon offer free cooked meals for families in crisis. We also provide onsite catering and event catering.

Our love of food and assisting others to reach their goals keeps us motivated. Chef and I are like an old married couple in our approach to our work. We have fun and support each other on challenging days.

My biggest challenges are turning my brain off, finding like-minded people to connect with and staying away from the computer when I need to take a break. It is too easy when you work from home to have work time run into personal time.

My marketing is mainly face to face. It is easy to talk about what we do and be enthusiastic. We have an active Facebook page where we post most of what we do. I always ask people to come see what we do and let the atmosphere, our jobseekers and our healthy wholesome food do the talking for us. I am confident cold-calling and just rocking up on someone's doorstep if that's what I need to do. Coffee meetings are great for a relaxed approach, so I can tell the story of how we operate, letting people know we use rescued foods, have four compost bins and well fed chickens. Our aim is to minimise waste.

With regard to work/life balance, family comes first. I have two grown-up children who have families of their own and are all passionate about food. I am solutions-orientated and organised, and though challenged sometimes when a family crisis happens, I can think through what I need to do and just do it. The boundaries between business and personal can become blurred, so I try to make some of my business activities pleasure, which is quite easy when working with food.

Some of my tips:

- Behaviour must be consistent
- Maintain boundaries
- Learn to say NO
- Build a support network. I use a combination of face to face, email, Skype, text
- Do what you love and are really passionate about
- Have at least three months' money in the bank
- Be prepared to learn and explore
- Just do it!

Christine Smith from Rowville Community Kitchen rowvillecommunitykitchen.com.au lives in Rowville, Victoria, Australia.

Live events

One of the best ways to supercharge your list-building is through live events. This would have to be the one tactic I have used that has paid huge dividends. When I first started a mailing list for my business, Content Marketing Cardiology, I had four subscribers. That quickly grew to more than 1000 after hosting live online events, including a telesummit and a few webinars.

Telesummits and teleseries

Telesummits are virtual events where you interview a number of speakers over an intense period, e.g. three days. Teleseries are similar, however they can stretch across several weeks. There are several models that work well for telesummits, and one of the most common is to offer the live interviews for free and charge a miniscule price to upgrade to a premium package that includes copies of all the recordings plus other bonuses. The advantage to upgrading is that your listeners don't have to attend live and can keep the recordings forever. To boost recording sales, the speakers and the host offer valuable free products that not only help them build their individual lists but also make it incredibly difficult for anyone to say no to the offer. Once the event is over, the recordings, transcripts and bonus items are made available to everyone who upgraded to the premium package. These can then be repurposed for other programs and products at a later time.

Webinars

Hosting a webinar is a terrific way to demonstrate your presentation style to potential clients and share your expertise. It gives you the opportunity to add a visual component that can make all the difference if you are teaching people how to do something.

Another approach is to offer free webinars in order to have the opportunity to talk about up-and-coming premium programs and services. There are a few different schools of thought about how these should be done. The way I approach this is to frame a free webinar as a sample class so people are in no doubt that I have a premium service on offer. I then give them my best content so they can see the value I offer.

At the beginning of the session, I ask my attendees for permission to share about my up-coming program and I let them know that I'll share that with them at the end of the webinar. I also make sure I have an irresistible offer that includes attendee discounts or special bonuses if they take up the offer. If they give their permission and hang around, they know to expect an offer. If they don't like the fact that I'm going to use the free webinar to promote a service that might be helpful for them, they can log off the webinar once the other content is finished.

A business is a business and at the end of the day, if you have a service that can help somebody get from point A to point B, then you are doing them a disservice by not making an offer. It really does boil down to your motivation and the way you go about it. If you leave any mention of the pitch right to the end, you'll annoy people, so it is better to broach the elephant in the room from the get-go.

If you want to avoid pitching at all in webinars, simply charge a fee for every webinar you present.

There are many webinar platforms, including Google Hangouts and gotowebinar.com. Shop around and find one that works for you. You can also create pre-recorded webinars for udemy.com.

Guest speaking at networking events

Once you start to establish yourself as the go-to person in your niche and develop a good speaking style to communicate your message, you'll find that invitations to speak at various networking events will flow freely. Networking event organisers need a fresh supply of qualified, engaging speakers for their events, so if you are prepared to speak for free or for a minimal fee, you can use the opportunity to build your list and build your reputation as a speaker. You will also have an opportunity to present a special offer for attendees and build your income. Recently I spoke at a networking event and while I had only a small take-up of my offer on the day, I gained a new high-end client who was at the event. In the end it was a lucrative speaking engagement.

With face-to-face events, it's a good idea to have forms that attendees can fill out to join your mailing list. If you do make an offer, it pays to add urgency into the equation. People will be keen to sign up on the spot if your offer is incredibly value-laden and runs out when the event ends. A note of caution here is to ensure your offer is valuable and not just hype. If you have been an engaging speaker, you won't need to manipulate people to sign up. They will be compelled to do so by the quality and value you offer.

Action Steps

Resolve to incorporate a live event into your marketing calendar within the next 12 months.

Make a to-do list of what you'll need to get the ball rolling. Who can you collaborate with to make this happen?

Un-Career Story

The following story illustrates how speaking at live events can propel your business forward.

Susan's Story

SP Communications operates as a specialist marketing and communications consultancy for the professional services sectors. We provide a variety of services including social media advice and management, public relations, marketing, copywriting, website and graphic design. I have two daughters, currently aged seven and four and they are the light and love of my life (except the occasional moments when they are driving me insane). I feel blessed to have them and my husband. We're a happy, tight-knit bunch who love to share a laugh and some silliness.

The catalyst for making the change from the corporate world to one of business owner was the realisation that no matter how hard I worked, how late I stayed or how experienced I was in my role at the time, I had effectively been sidelined onto the 'mummy track' where there was no chance of promotion, progress or further training.

From what I could see, it was because I worked four days a week (the horror of not doing the full five days, even though my four days were 12 hours long most days). The standard 40 hours per week at your desk is such an antiquated way of working. It doesn't prove your knowledge or experience. So three years after I had my first child, I planted the seeds of self-employment, setting up my business and balancing the corporate world with late nights, ensuring SP Communications had a viable start.

It was a tough time handling two kids and two jobs, and it stretched me in ways I wouldn't have thought possible, but as I sit here telling you this, I can wholeheartedly say it was worth it! Two years after the first seed was planted, my first child was five and starting school, and my second child was two. I finally made my exit and I have never looked back!

I thrive on the dynamic nature of my business. You always have to be on top of your client's business and their competitive landscapes and there is always something new to learn or someone new to meet. I am also motivated by my kids and my mum. My mum inspires me, she and my dad came to this country with one suitcase and built a life. My kids make me want to better myself all the time as I believe the ethos that kids learn from what you do, not what you say. They need to see it to be it. And if I can help my girls become strong and independent women I will be one happy mum!

I'm lucky that word of mouth does most of the marketing for my business these days. However, I also do a mix of speaking events, article writing, guest columns, seminars, attend networking events and social media.

I have to say my biggest challenge is trusting my gut instinct when it comes to business decisions. Over time I have become more comfortable with it, however I do believe that being a business owner tests your self and personality just as much, if not more than your skill sets. Trusting that you are making the right decisions for your business with regards to who you work with, or how you overcome the testing times of starting up, or just how you bounce back after a trying day, says more about you and impacts your business just as much as everything else. You can't just shut the door or leave the office and forget about your bad day. Your business is your baby; it never stops impacting you.

There are good days and bad days. I create a working week that is a mix of long work days and shorter ones that enable me to be there for school pick ups and extra-curricular activities. However, the shorter work days are buffered by long nights at the computer. I'm a night owl though, so it works well for me.

If I could share one tip it's this: ditch the guilt. There are days the laundry will overtake the house, the kids will eat noodles for the fourth day in a row or conversely, you have not completed your work to-do list. You know what? Don't worry about it. Don't feel guilty. Being a business owner is HARD YAKKA. Tomorrow's another day, try again then. Women have to remember we're not infallible, but we also need to know that we're stronger than we realise, and we will get to our goals, we just have more kids toys, shoes and other stuff to step over to get there!

If you're going to leave your job to start a business, make sure your business is viable. Do your research. Start small if you can, while you're still working, especially if you rely on your income for household purposes. You can use this time to organise your website, business cards and potentially get a few sales or several regular clients depending on what your business is. And when you are ready to take the plunge, give yourself a deadline for success. I set myself the goal to cover my corporate income within 12 months of starting up, as a measure of business viability. It's important to set goals and test out your business.

Also, a support network is invaluable. Talking to other business owners is so important as they understand your challenges and are a great to learn from. Mostly, have faith in yourself and your abilities. And when you get frustrated or are having another sleepless night at the PC, remember you're not alone. We've all been there and come through the other side and so shall you.

Susan Popovski from SP Communications
spcommunications.com.au lives in Sydney, New South Wales, Australia.

Landing pages

Landing pages are pages on your website that contain nothing else but your case for why a prospective client should buy from you, or opt-in to your mailing list, and a link to do this.

Long-copy landing pages, which have a prolific amount of information about the product, can work if done well. They enable the potential buyer to take in every scrap of information and allow you to make a compelling and in-depth argument for purchase. They don't work when they are too long, or if the price is concealed. Like any marketing copy, they need to be well written and have high quality, original images.

A good landing page will do the following:

- Catch the reader's attention quickly in the first headline
- Spell out the pain points (ie. issues that cause worry or concern) for the reader

- Share how you can take them from the problems they have to where they want to be - the outcomes for them

- Provide a rundown of exactly how you'll do that

- Provide real testimonials from happy clients

- Provide a clear and easy to find price. Three price alternatives generally work well

Be aware that many people will scroll right down to the bottom to see the price and then go back and read through everything in detail.

A tactic I've used is to insert an anchor into the first section of the landing page to take someone directly to the price. This is not only helpful but builds trust as you are acknowledging their priorities. People feel less manipulated when you are not afraid to tell them how much something will cost them. Of course you still need to back up that price by spelling out the incredible value it offers.

A landing page does not have to be long. However it does have to be focused on the benefits for the reader. Your potential clients could care less about your state of the art technology. What they really want to know is how your product will help them get from problem to solution.

Action Steps

Create a landing page for one of your products or services, or engage the services of a copywriter and web designer who can help you with this, if you don't feel writing sales copy and designing landing pages is your thing.

Bonus: Download bonus resources that dig deeper into this topic. For this chapter, I interviewed Phil McGregor, Facebook Ads specialist, speaker and serial entrepreneur. There's also a free Email Marketing Funnel Template and a printable affirmation to inspire you to take action now. To access these bonus resources, simply sign up here: bit.ly/uncareerresources

Chapter 11

Overcoming overwhelm and psychological barriers to success

Juggling business and life

One of the primary reasons people establish their own business is so they can work around their families and lifestyles, and enjoy more flexibility. There are some big advantages to working for yourself. Parents can work around the school schedule and enjoy more family time. For those who aren't parents, working for yourself means greater flexibility. Well, at least in theory.

The reality can be far from what this ideal picture paints, depending on the nature of your business. The truth is that many startup businesses require a lot of work, especially at the beginning, and this can mean long hours, early mornings and late nights. If you run a hobby business, you're probably not too concerned with profits and scaling your business growth. However, if you are an entrepreneur establishing a business to create a sustainable income, you may find keeping the balance between work and family more challenging.

There have been times in my journey when I've lain in bed wondering what on earth I am doing all this for. I long to take off into the sunset with my boys and a tent in tow. I wish I had more freedom to enjoy just being a mum. At times like this, I feel suffocated and trapped by my un-career choice. That's when the 'I don't want to do this anymore' monster senses my vulnerability and attacks.

Usually when the monster attacks, it's after a very late night working on my business. I creep to bed so I don't wake up my family, and the house is so quiet you can hear the cat purring in the next room.

I like the solitude of late nights when I have a lot of work to get done, but sometimes my body aches and I wonder what happened to the day. If I get a few days like that in a row, that's when the 'I don't want to do this anymore' monster goes on the prowl.

I know that when the monster comes calling, it's time to rethink my priorities. It's time to get out of the house and go for a long walk, and time to get some help with the things that the 'I don't want to do this anymore' monster feeds on.

When you are passionate about your business, it is hard to stop, and if you're not careful, things like family activities, cleaning the house, gardening, doing the grocery shopping and preparing meals can take a back seat. I know, from personal experience, that it doesn't feel good to work in a neglected environment.

It is also a good idea to set aside time for connecting with your family. If work is interfering with family life to the extent that you aren't able to do your usual activities together, that's a massive red flag that changes need to be made, particularly if you work from home. Sometimes it takes a little extra effort to create clearer lines between work and family time.

- Choose to turn off the mobile or computer after a certain time of day and on weekends

- Get together with other friends to prepare a bunch of family meals so that cooking doesn't take up as much time and you are spending precious time with friends

- Take regular breaks from the computer and plan your time on social media by writing a schedule of posts for the week

Looking after you

It is easy to forget to look after yourself when you work for yourself. Here's a list of some self-care ideas you might want to put higher on the priority list. Don't attempt them all and add to your workload, just pick a couple to help keep your battery charged:

- Eat a balanced diet of whole foods

- Exercise regularly

- Take the time to make health care appointments for yourself

- Get your hair cut

- Book a massage on a regular basis if you can. You'll be amazed at how much better you feel

- Read a book just for the sake of it

- Watch TV or listen to talk back radio

- Enjoy your garden

- Visit with friends or family

Supporting each other

Use your online networks to get to know other people who run their own micro or home based business in your area, and together you can support each other in a number of ways:

- Get together for a coffee and a play-date at a local play café or pub with a playground

- Offer to support each other with child-minding and use a points system to keep track of who has taken this up and who has helped out

- Collaborate on list-building and page-building promotions

- Don't forget to outsource when you can to avoid burn out

Dealing with a negative partner, friend or family member

Other people's issues don't have to rule your life. When you let them go, you'll feel so much better.

Sometimes the growth and change that happens in your life as a result of starting your own business can leave your loved ones feeling left behind in the wake of your determination. It can be hard for them to understand just what working for yourself means to you. If they are saying things that leave you feeling bad about starting your own business, it's time to turn that on its head and start communicating how you feel.

Sometimes hurtful comments come from a place of feeling left out or neglected. Sometimes all it takes is a listening and empathetic ear to break through the words and get to the core issue bothering the other person.

Sometimes, though, the other person may be stuck in a different paradigm where work means doing the daily grind in a nine-to-five job. The thought that work can be fun is foreign to people who are comfortable being worker bees, who think that work has to be hard, long and unenjoyable.

I struggled to have my work taken seriously, until I started making enough money to pay tax. I noticed the complaints stopped when there was greater income, but it didn't make me feel much better. I still felt misunderstood and undervalued. I realised that I had to stop relying on external validation to feel good about my business. I had to let anyone who had flung criticism my way, off the hook.

If you love what you do, and it makes you happy, communicating with those who don't really get it can make the difference between feeling crappy and feeling understood. Who wants to waste energy on addressing negative Nellies? I sure don't.

If you're really struggling with the opinions of others about your business, don't forget to jump onto forums and social media communities for moral support. Other people's issues don't have to rule your life. When you let them go, you'll feel so much better.

Dealing with your change in identity

Some entrepreneurs leave high flying careers behind, and while they may find the change exhilarating and wear their new title as founder/principal/owner as a badge of honour, some struggle with the loss of their former identities, their social life in the office and even the office politics. It is natural to grieve the loss of the life you once had, but don't let that define you or hold you back as you move forward into your new venture. When I first started offering cooking and cleaning services through Mumatopia, I struggled with the whole concept of providing domestic services. In my mind they were menial jobs but in my heart I knew they were a very important part of the business concept I had. I had to get over myself and my prejudices towards different work roles. If you're struggling with your new identity or grieving your former one, I urge you to talk to a counsellor to work through these issues so they don't hold you back.

Un-Career Story

The following story below is a great example of the challenges women face when it comes to work/life balance.

Celena's Story

I was a senior state government officer when I left the corporate world. The arrival of my first grandchild was what lead me to make a lifestyle and career change. I didn't want to work full time while my daughter was on maternity leave as I wanted to be there for her. Also, the government offered a package which would provide me with the equivalent of around a year and a half pay if I was working part time. It provided me with the opportunity to grow my business as a celebrant. I could not let go of my years of business development knowledge and experience so I also started a business development program for small businesses, which has now morphed into a business that helps people with the transition to semi or full retirement.

I now juggle child care for my grandchildren, care for my elderly mum, life with my retired husband and both businesses.

My background in government helped me get started. I still have some very valuable media contacts locally and have a highly regarded profile and reputation. Social media is fantastic also, when you use it correctly. I work odd hours from home, so having flexibility is a huge plus.

It's not been all smooth sailing. Although the celebrant work absolutely took off, I struggled with letting go of the high profile, achiever, influencer, queen networker in me. I left my corporate role without really considering how the change would affect me on a personal level. I have experienced so many emotions since leaving, so my advice is make time to speak to a business advisor to discuss issues such as family needs and how to rebrand yourself as an independent business owner. How will you cope when you are introduced without a title, or one that is so far removed from who you have been?

For me, as a senior state government officer, to be introduced as a celebrant was a huge change. In starting a new business you need to consider how much you want and need to earn, what your drivers and passions are and how you might use these for a small business. These may have nothing to do with what you actually trained for and worked at in your career! There are many people who, in leaving the corporate world and starting a new business, also relocate interstate to their dream new life away from family and lifelong friends. My suggestion is perhaps rent rather than sell your home to see if that place you always loved to holiday in really is the place for you to live permanently.

My biggest challenge is time. It is difficult to juggle work with personal commitments. I get pulled by the needs of others and really struggle for some 'me' time. I have cut back on the wedding work to give me time to assist my daughter with her babies and have a bit more time for myself. Also, as I age, being relevant with current business network groups is also a challenge. Fortunately my work as a celebrant covers all age groups—hatch, match and dispatch!

Celena Ross from Retiree Matters, Women Redefining Retirement, retireematters.com.au from The Sunshine Coast, Queensland, Australia

Seven keys to overcoming psychological barriers to success

If you're lacking motivation or feeling self-sabotage is rearing its ugly head, try these tips that helped me push through when I've felt overwhelmed or over it.

1. Assess your motivations daily

"You know you are on the road to success if you would do your job, and not be paid for it."

Oprah Winfrey

It's easy to get side-tracked on the path to business success, so it's a good idea to understand and be aware of what is driving your decisions. Sometimes we make decisions based on fear, ego or peer pressure. Sometimes the fear is the fear of missing out on an opportunity and sometimes it's fear of failure. Sometimes we're attracted to opportunities because they feel good or make us look good. Sometimes we feel compelled to take up an opportunity or make a decision because everybody else seems to be doing it. When faced with decisions and opportunities, take a nano-second to ask yourself what's really going on. Is it the right call for you? Is it going to lead you further down the road to achieving your goals? Be really honest with yourself.

Understanding what motivates you to go down a particular path and being in control of your destiny is important, not only for your personal development but for your business success.

Ask yourself on a daily basis: am I doing this because I can't not do it, because I love it and can't wait for the alarm to go off in the morning, or am I doing this because everybody else is doing it, because someone told me I should, because I feel I have to, or because it seemed like a good idea at the time?

If what you are doing is not going to lead you towards your goals, is not something you enjoy and is following someone else's agenda, then perhaps you need to reassess your motivations and the direction you are heading in.

2. Set your intentions for each day and write them as though they've already happened

"Every achiever I have ever met says, 'My life turned around when I began to believe in me.'"

Robert Schuller

If you are prone to distraction, starting your day by jotting down what you want to achieve can really kick your productivity into gear.

Rather than writing a 'to-do' list, try writing a few intentions down as if they have already happened. When you do this, it changes your mindset from thinking about what you yet have to do to being grateful for what you have already achieved, even if you haven't yet achieved it. It is a powerful motivator to help you move through procrastination, because, in your mind you're already committed to the task.

For example, 'I am grateful that I managed to get my bookkeeping up-to-date today and I feel lighter as a result!' is stronger than 'I will get my bookkeeping up-to-date today'.

Setting your intention sets the tone for how you want your day to go and keeps you focused on what you need to do.

3. Ask yourself 'Who am I not to?'

"Whether you think you can, or think you can't, you're right."

Henry Ford

We all have a choice in how we respond, not only to the doubts leveraged against us by others, but the doubts we leverage against ourselves.

Is your brilliance being diminished by thoughts of failure or inadequacy?

Women are living in an incredible age of empowerment. They are starting up more businesses than ever before and are leading the way in education, in philanthropy and in the tuck shops and scout dens in every community.

Women are rejecting the corporate world and going solo in increasing numbers in order to enjoy better quality of life with their families. However, women can be their own worst enemies when it comes to undermining their worth and value.

We all have a choice in how we respond, not only to the doubts leveraged against us by others, but the doubts we leverage against ourselves.

We all have trigger points that alert us when we're moving out of our comfort zones. Sometimes we sabotage ourselves, because to go beyond where we are feels unnatural and scary. But moving out of our comfort zone can be good. It means we're growing.

If you're feeling stuck, overwhelmed or trapped, start imagining a different existence, one where you are moving forward, one where you have the balance right between work and family, and one where you are free to live your dream.

By imagining, you make the doing more likely. It all starts with you.

The next time you start to feel that 'Who am I to…?' thinking creep in, replace that thought with 'Who am I not to?'

By imagining, you make the doing more likely. It all starts with you.

The limits you place on yourself are artificial. They're made up, so get rid of them! Why shouldn't it be you who... climbs Mt Everest, bungy jumps off a bridge, runs an international telesummit or kick-starts a new International Day of Mumpreneurs? Why shouldn't it be you who gets the interview with the journalist or speaks at a conference? You don't need to wait for someone else to have all the good ideas and good fortune. Value yourself and ask 'Who am I not to...?'

The Knots Prayer

Dear God,

Please untie the knots
that are in my mind,
my heart and my life.
Remove the have nots,
the can nots and the do nots
that I have in my mind.

Erase the will nots,
may nots,
might nots that may find
a home in my heart.

Release me from the could nots,
would nots and
should nots that obstruct my life.

And most of all,
dear God,
I ask that you remove from my mind,
my heart and my life all of the am nots
that I have allowed to hold me back,
especially the thought
that I am not good enough.
Amen

Anonymous Poem

Un-Career Story

In the following story, Robin shares some tips for dealing with negative self-talk.

Robin's Story

I had been an executive assistant to vice presidents, directors and other executives for 13 years. I was tired of the disrespect and management taking my ideas as their own, and was making less than my peers in the company, so I decided to start my own business. I had wanted my own business since I was a kid, and my husband told me, "If you want to build a business, do it! I support you 100%."

That was all I needed and I jumped from a salaried job into being an entrepreneur. It has been such an amazing journey. In the beginning, it was scary to go from a pay cheque to 'what's next?', however ten years later I don't look back. It is amazing to have the freedom to create whatever I want.

I started off as a business coach, teaching women how to build a business. Soon we needed to hire support for them. We tried to find solid virtual assistants (VAs) that had integrity, and they were few and far between. One of my clients said "Why don't you just do it, you taught us! Who better?"

So my husband and I sat down and talked it out. We decided there were thousands of business coaches and limited great VAs, so I re-invented the business. Since making that change I have created a referral-based practice supporting other women entrepreneurs. I also started training women to start their own virtual assistant businesses. I have been able to watch women grow a business that replaced their pay cheques in as little as six months. Talk about rewarding! I have taken my clients from making $150k a year to over $1.5m a year. It is exciting to watch so much success happen and be a part of it. My next step is building a team that will support a larger group of entrepreneurs!

My most effective marketing has been word of mouth, which has been very powerful. I take care of my clients and they talk about me. I use Facebook as my main social platform, and have made many solid relationships and connections there. I also attend live events and connect with people face to face. It's nice when the face-to-face meshes with Facebook. You don't know how many times I have gone to an event and had people come up to me because they met me on Facebook. It's all about connecting.

The biggest challenges are those that try to verbally destroy you, sometimes out of fear and sometimes out of jealousy. The key is to stay focused on your goal and find a solid support system to keep you on track. Then there is your own 'monkey chatter', as I call it, the negative talk that goes on in your head. My advice is to get a stuffed monkey, and when the chatter happens chuck it across the room. It's amazing how quickly the noise stops.

When it comes to juggling priorities, it is all about balance. Working from home makes it tougher. There are so many distractions. I have a separate room for the office. That way I can walk away from my work. I take mini-breaks during the day to engage with my fur babies and chat with hubby on his lunch break. The key is not forgetting to take care of you while building the business, stay focused and remain accountable. What inspires me to keep going is the people I am around and support. There is something about being a catalyst for success. Plus I do something I love, so I want to get up every day and do it.

If you're thinking about establishing your own business, I would say that unless your current income is not needed for the family unit to survive, keep your job and start building the business on the side. You could go part time. Just keep some money flowing in. If you have another income in the house that can meet your needs, then go for it!

Don't give up! Remember what you do today affects you 60 to 90 days from today. Keep going! Most folks quit just before they make it. Also, run away from anything that says 'buy in and we guarantee you will make XX dollars'. No one can guarantee you will make money. You need to invest in training and coaching, but if they promise a certain amount of money it probably is a scam.

Robin Hardy from Integrity Virtual Services
integrityvirtualservices.com lives in York, South Carolina, USA.

4. Understand that what you have to give is unique

There is no one person in the world who is quite like you. Find the music you love and get boogying!

My children have a favourite book from when they were little, called *Giraffes Can't Dance*. In the book the giraffe decries his lack of dancing ability but in the end, he discovers that he has his own unique style. He declares that, "We all can dance… when we find the music that we love".

When you start to feel overwhelmed, or 'not good enough', take some time out to remind yourself that you are brilliant, amazing and unique—because you truly are. There is no one person in the world who is quite like you. Find the music you love and get boogying!

Stop worrying about what everyone else is doing or whether people are copying you. Even if someone copied your business concept and took your words, they can never really copy you. You are completely unique. Your story is unique and your ideas came from your own unique perspective. Nobody can take that away from you.

Plaster affirmations on the wall, fridge and bathroom mirror if you have to, but don't let a day go by without you saying to yourself, "I am an incredible individual, unique and beautiful. I can do anything I set my mind to".

Your differences make your point of difference. Embrace them and love them, for they give you an incredible gift, the ability to deliver your own products and services in your own unique way.

5. Let the past stay in the past

"You are now at a crossroads. This is your opportunity to make the most important decision you will ever make. Forget your past. Who are you now? Who have you decided you really are now? Don't think about who you have been. Who are you now? Who have you decided to become? Make this decision consciously. Make it carefully. Make it powerfully."

Anthony Robbins

As a child I was tortured and tormented for my looks, my tenacity and even my gumption.

As a child, I was a 'different' kid. I didn't fit the mould and so, until quite recently, when I looked at photos of myself as a little girl, it brought up lots of negative emotions that I associated with being a skinny, feisty little girl. One girl's mother told me I'd probably end up in jail one day and another, exasperated at my hyper behaviour as a young child, said that she didn't think I'd ever amount to anything. As an adult, I've wasted a lot of energy trying to prove my worth through accomplishments. I now know that I don't need to prove anything to anyone.

As a child, I kept getting into trouble for doing the wrong thing when I didn't mean to. I learned to apologise, not so I could express my sorrow, but as a way to avoid conflict. As an adult, it has meant that my discernment radar is sometimes not so finely tuned, and I've often apologised for things even when I really shouldn't have. I now know that I am not always in the wrong and can look at situations more objectively.

As a child I was picked on and bullied physically and psychologically. I learned to suffer in silence and put up with others' abusive behaviour. As an adult it's meant that I have still tolerated abuse rather than understanding that I didn't deserve to be treated that way. I now know that abusive behaviour is not acceptable and have chosen a different path for my life.

As a child, I learned that standing out from the crowd meant you were selfish or self-centred. As an adult, I have struggled with being in the spotlight. Part of me loves it, because I love the adrenalin of standing on a stage or using the media to get the word out about something important. I love the feeling of making a difference for someone. However, part of me wants to sabotage my success, because it feels more familiar to listen to those voices from my past that said I wasn't good enough. I now know that being in the spotlight is a great place to be, even if it's outside of my comfort zone.

I share these examples with you not to gain your sympathy, but to show you how our perception of ourselves as children can carry through to our adult years in ways we might not expect.

The only way you can move forward is to process and make peace with your past, and to not wear it around your neck like a millstone. Forgive those who have hurt you, and then thank them for what they taught you. This will allow you to grow into who you are now.

Your past and the words people have spoken about you in your life don't have to define who you are now. You have the power to define who you are. You have the power to respond to triggers differently.

The past is the past. Learn from it, embrace what it gave you, say thanks for the lessons you learned and move forward, free from its chains.

6. Stop being a perfectionist

As a solo business owner, it can be tempting to feel that everything needs to be perfect, because it all reflects directly back to you. The funny thing is, when you do make a mistake, and we all do, if you admit your faux pas and share your learning journey through blog posts and emails, you will usually find that your readers respond positively rather than negatively.

People can relate to someone who is human and who tries and fails, picks themselves up and tries again. If you aim for perfection in every instance, it will stop you from moving forward.

Now, I'm not advocating putting out products or services that are poor quality. It's just that your idea of perfect might be vastly different from others. You can waste a lot of time stuffing about with a blog post or giving an image an extra nip and tuck, but really, the product or service you had on offer three hours earlier was good enough.

If the need to do everything perfectly is standing in your way, practise aiming for good enough. Hit 'publish' on that blog post, then go back later and tweak anything that is still bothering you. That way you can get on with what is really important and not get bogged down in pointless activity.

7. Don't give up

"Most people give up just when they are about to achieve success. They quit on the one yard line. They give up at the last minute of the game one foot from a winning touchdown."

Ross Perot

The past is the past. Learn from it, embrace what it gave you, say thanks for the lessons you learned and move forward, free from its chains.

When I was younger, I loved listening to and reading about my grandparents' journey to Australia. As a young Jewish boy living in a country that discriminated against Jews, my grandpa had to go way above and beyond to succeed. He had to work hard to get the best grades so he'd qualify for a scholarship to the best schools, and then had to be within the top one percent of students just to get into university. During his time at university, he had to avoid things like Jew-bashing days, and work hard to ensure he could leave university, not only with his face intact, but with grades high enough to get into his chosen profession, engineering. My grandpa was someone who never gave up, even in the face of terrible adversity.

About the time he left university, the great depression hit, and in order to secure a paid position he first had to offer to work for free. After doing that for a few months, he was eventually offered a paid position and quickly worked his way up the ranks. However as anti-Semitism grew, his chances of furthering his career in Hungary diminished. Little did he know what was to come for most of his family during the war. In the months before Hitler marched into Eastern Europe, my grandpa knew that his family's best chance was to get out of Hungary, so he sold everything he had, bought diamonds, stuffed them into the end of his fountain pen and moved his young family to Australia.

When my grandparents arrived in Australia, they had to start from scratch, learn a new language and re-invent themselves. Because they were Hungarian, they were treated as enemy aliens the first few years they were in Australia, during World War Two. Once it was realised what Hitler was doing to the Jews in Europe, my grandparents' lives became easier, but they had lost touch with all family members inside Hungary as their letters were being censored and returned to them.

My grandmother, who had a Masters in Physics and was known as one of the most prominent mathematicians in 20th century Australia, continued as a maths teacher, a highly educated working mum in an era when working while raising a family was frowned upon. She taught at a prestigious girl's school in Adelaide that spawned some of the country's great women leaders. Both my grandparents were prize winners in the famed Eötvös national mathematics and physics competitions in Hungary.

When I think about the hardships I've faced in life, I only have to think about my grandparents to realise what an easy path I have had. Everything they achieved was done so with great determination and struggle. These two incredible individuals taught me to never give up.

All business ventures come with days that make you wonder if it's worth it.

There have been many points in my entrepreneurial journey where I've felt like throwing in the towel. When I began supporting women in childbirth, I'd come home from some births feeling defeated and traumatised by the way hospital staff treated my client or me.

But then, a text would arrive from my client saying how much she valued me being there for her and how she felt she couldn't have done it without me there for support. And when I visited my clients afterwards, and saw they were travelling well and their babies were well and happy, it made it all worth it.

All business ventures come with days that make you wonder if it's worth it.

I've launched programs that didn't fly, invested hours with little return, and have felt undervalued by the very people I was trying to help.

Not giving up doesn't necessarily mean doing the same thing, living the same way or repeating the same patterns over and over again. If you keep plugging away in the same way, nothing will change. It might mean changing direction. Make mistakes, sure, but learn from them and move forward quickly.

Not giving up means being resourceful and innovative, and sometimes the best ideas come from your failures.

If what you really want out of life is to be financially independent, to step off the corporate ladder and to be free from the trappings that come with old-fashioned ideas of success, then you owe it to yourself and those you love to go for your dreams.

At the end of the day, you are the only person standing in your way! So what are you waiting for? Start on the path to your brilliant un-career.

Bonus: Download bonus resources that dig deeper into this topic. For this chapter, I interviewed Sally Thibault, speaker, author of David's Gift and EFT practitioner. There's also a free Self Care Checklist and a printable affirmation to inspire you to look after yourself better now. To access these bonus resources, simply sign up here: bit.ly/uncareerresources

Bibliography

Cohoon, J. McGrath, Wadhwa, Vivek and Mitchell, Lesa, Are Successful Women Entrepreneurs Different from Men? (May 11, 2010). P 4. Available at SSRN: ssrn.com/abstract=1604653 (cited in Chapter 1)

Growing Under The Radar: An exploration of the achievements of million-dollar women-owned firms, Amex Open Forum, 2013. d8a8a12b527478184df8-1fd282026c3ff4ae711d11ecc95a1d47.ssl.cf1.rackcdn. com/wp-content/uploads/2013/07/GrowingUndertheRadar_Full-Report.pdf

Clark, M., Eaton, M., Lind, W., Pye, E., and Bateman, L. (2011). Key Statistics: Australian Small Business. Australian Department of Innovation Industry, Science and Research. Commonwealth of Australia, Canberra.

Jayasekera, Ranadeva, 'Small Can Be Vulnerable': Failure Prediction of Unlisted Companies (June 22, 2011). SIBR. Available at SSRN: ssrn.com/abstract=1869431

Porat, M. U. (1977). The Information Economy: Definition and Measurement. Superintendent of Documents, US Government Printing Office, Washington DC. USA.

Mollick, Ethan R., The Dynamics of Crowdfunding: Determinants of Success and Failure (July 25, 2012). Available at SSRN: ssrn.com/abstract=2088298

Bygrave, William D., Lange, Julian, Mollov, Aleksandar, Pearlmutter, Michael and Singh, Sunil , Pre-Startup Formal Business Plans and Post-Startup Performance: A Study of 116 New Ventures (September, 17 2008). Venture Capital Journal, Vol. 9, No. 4, pp. 1-20, October 2007; Babson College Center for Entrepreneurship Research Paper No. 2008-8. Available at SSRN: ssrn.com/abstract=1269484

www.sba.gov found via www.forbes.com/sites/jasonnazar/2013/09/09/16-surprising-statistics-about-small-businesses/

smallbiztrends.com/2012/12/start-up-failure-rates-the-definitive-numbers.html

www.nielsen.com/us/en/reports/2012/state-of-the-media-the-social-media-report-2012.html